MAKING MONEY

FEES FOR LIBRARY SERVICES

ALICE SIZER WARNER

NEAL-SCHUMAN
PUBLISHERS, INC.
NEW YORK   LONDON

Published by Neal-Schuman Publishers, Inc.
23 Leonard Street
New York, NY 10013

Copyright © by Alice Sizer Warner

Printed and bound in the United States of America

Library of Congress Cataloging-in-Publication Data

Warner, Alice Sizer.
  Making money.

  Includes index.
  1. Library finance.   2. Library fines and fees.
3. Information services—Fees.   4. Reference services
(Libraries)—Fees.   I. Title.
Z683.W37 1989   025.5'24   88-12501
ISBN 1-55570-053-5

Contents

Acknowledgments   v
Preface   vii

1 CONTROVERSY   1
Fee vs. Free: Conscientious Librarians' Dilemma   2
Should We or Shouldn't We   4
Who Sells What, to Whom, for How Much?   6
The Stress Factor   10

2 ACTIVITY   15
Fee-Based Services in Academic Libraries   15
Fee-Based Service in Public Libraries   20
Fees Charged by Specialized Libraries   23
Fees Charged by Medical Libraries   24
Fees Charged by Association Libraries   27
Charging Back   29
Charging Out   34

3 PLANNING   43
What are the Goals of the Service?   44
What Services will be Sold?   48
Who Will Buy Fee-Based Services?   50
How Will the Service be Organized   53
How Do We Handle the Money Earned?   56
Do We Have the Money for Planning and Startup?   61
How Will Fees Be Set?   63
What About Scheduling and Timing?   70
Forecasts?   71

How Do We Handle Ethical Issues?   72
Confidentiality?   73
Liability?   73
When Is a Profit Not for Profit?   74
What to Do About Copyright?   76

4   IMPLEMENTING   87
The Proposal: Selling the Plan to Decision Makers   87
Selling the Plan to Library Staff   90
Planning for and Shifting to Chargebacks/Chargeouts   90

5   CLIENTS AND CUSTOMERS   99
Current Situation   100
How to Make Selling Easy   104
Following the Rules   105

6   SELLING   113
Selling for Free: Low-Budget Activities   113
Brochures   121
Advertising, Exhibiting   128
Direct Mail   131
Marketing Within: Chargebacks   134

Afterword   141
Index   145

Acknowledgments

This book was created by dozens of people; without them, there would be no book.

Initial seeds were planted in Ann Arbor, Michigan, in May 1987. Co-attendees at a conference on fee-based services in academic libraries felt that a beginner's, practical, how-to-get-started book was needed and they encouraged this author to try to create one. They would help, they said, and they did. Conference chairperson Anne Beaubien of University of Michigan's MITS (Michigan Information Transfer Source) was especially encouraging. Other fee-based service veterans at that conference inspired and assisted and nudged the book along, especially Fran Wood from University of Wisconsin, Miriam Drake from Georgia Institute of Technology, and Mary McNierny Grant from C.W. Post in New York.

Patricia Glass Schuman of Neal-Schuman Publishers also urged creation of this book. Her colleague, Jack Neal, guided the book from first attempts to publication. Editor Andrea Pedolsky skillfully cajoled and strengthened.

Early drafts were reviewed by Fran Wood, by Mary Grant, and by Mary Pensyl of the Computerized Literature Search Service at the Massachusetts Institute of Technology, all of whom contributed substantially.

Helen Witzenhausen of John Wiley and Sons, Inc., gave thoughtful critique from a special librarian's point of view. Barbara Felicetti, formerly of InfoMotion, commented as an information entrepreneur looking at information intrapreneuring.

Alexandra Baker applied her writing skills with a red

pencil that shortened paragraphs, eliminated commas, and generally upgraded my use of the English language.

Special thanks go to Judith Monteux who paid attention to other papers on my desk so I could pay attention to this book.

Caleb Warner, as always, did most.

Thank you, all.

Preface

This is a first book, a primer. If you are exploring fee-based activity in your library, read this book *before* telephoning or writing or visiting your colleagues in the fee-charging world to plague them with questions. *Making Money* provides a basic introduction to fee charging as well as to the phenomenon of charging back library costs to departments or projects within an organization.

This book is presented as a companion to another book I wrote on charging fees for information service—*Mind Your Own Business: A Guide for the Information Entrepreneur*, also published by Neal-Schuman. *Mind Your Own Business* is about information entrepreneurs. This one is about information intrapreneurs—about charging fees *within* an institution. It is based on my experiences over the last 15 years as a consultant, on my readings, and on conversations I've had with colleagues working in institutions charging fees or charging back for information *services*.

This is not a book about overdue fines, copy machine coins, or rental of best sellers or videocassette recordings. What you will read is a description of what is currently happening in North American libraries regarding charging for library and information services, a discussion about charging back and charging out, detailed guidelines for planning a fee-based service, and specific suggestions about marketing and selling.

This is not an operating manual of how to manage an ongoing fee-based service on a day-to-day, year-after-year, basis. That book waits to be written.

Instead, administrators struggling with go-or-no-go decision-making will be exposed to what might be involved should fee-based service become reality, librarians starting fee-based service will find how-to guidance, and librarians in institutions whose activity is being, or may be, charged back within the institution to departments or projects or jobs will find some suggestions on how to make this work. While this book obviously cannot provide all the answers it can give a few, and it can suggest what further questions to ask.

Almost 500 questionnaires were sent out. Among those receiving questionnaires were head librarians in Fortune 100 companies and librarians in a dozen public libraries identified as having fee-based services. Attendees at the 1987 Ann Arbor conference on fee-based information services received questionnaires as did selected individuals listed on an American Library Association FISCAL (Fee-based Information Service Centers in Academic Libraries) mailing list. Also included were those who had recently attended one of more than a dozen sessions of my one-day continuing education workshop, "Making Money: Fees for Information Service."

Almost 20 percent of those individuals receiving questionnaires were generous enough to reply, and more people telephoned to express their views. Several others asked to be included and, of course, their ideas and suggestions were warmly welcomed.

All stories in this book are true. Quotations, advice and contributions throughout the book are from actual, if perforce unidentified, sources. Only library names and individuals' names, but not their experiences, have been rigidly held in confidence. All who responded to this book's questionnaire were promised anonymity, and this has been honored.

Reasons for shielding identities are many. First of all, it is natural to be franker, to be more open, knowing that what you say is guaranteed not to come back to haunt you. There are happy, successful people as well as frustrated, confused and unhappy people working in fee-based environments. Blunt and conflicting opinions roam freely throughout this book, and

I feel this is more useful to readers than a compilation of politically laundered remarks.

Second, although some contributors insisted on anonymity, others didn't care, and a few wanted spotlights: keeping track of what preference was whose was awkward, fraught with possibility for error, and otherwise impossible to manage with either accuracy or grace.

Third, staff of existing fee-based services are literally plagued by those who seek personalized advice on how to do the same, or some variation of the same, in their own libraries. Since we are all human, those who ask the most questions seem to have done the least homework. We want you to read this book and to follow up on other sources indicated in this book *before* rattling your colleagues cages: have a heart, they're busy!

Fourth, and probably most important, is the fact that with time, things change: time lapsed between doing research for this book and writing this book, between manuscript submission and book production. By the time you read these words, many players' identities will have changed: it is what they did when they did, why they did it, how they did it, what they felt about what they did, and what they wished they had done instead that remain useful to us now.

Practicing library administrators, and not I, are qualified to decide whether, ethically, fees for information services should or should not be charged. For right or for wrong, decisions about fee-charging are being made daily, nationwide, by administrators in public libraries, academic libraries, and special libraries of all kinds. Probably the only exempt libraries are those for little school children, although undoubtedly the exception that proves the rule will soon crop up.

This much is painfully obvious: there is no one right way, there is no one-size-fits-all philosophy. There is no all-abiding rule to fit all libraries. We are all a little bit different.

One of the questions on the questionnaire for this book was, "What has been, for you, the hardest part of being involved in a fee-based service?" One librarian replied, "Not

hard, but certainly challenging, stimulating, frustrating, etc.
Working with this fee-based service has provided me with the
most exciting experience of my professional career."

May all of you who read this book have as much fun.

Alice Sizer Warner
Lexington, Massachusetts

1
Controversy

Fees for information service. To charge or not to charge? Solution, question, or moral dilemma? For some it is how, not whether. Others struggle with go-or-no-go decisions. Yet others, the most vocal, are ardent nay-sayers: for them this itch, if there is an itch at all, is most definitely, not divine. Fees for information service: this is not, by any stretch of imagination, a lukewarm issue.

Where librarians gather together debates about fees abound. Whole days are devoted to "What's a Fair Fare? The Service Fee Dilemma in Academic Libraries" or to "Information Brokering and Consulting: Inside and Out," or to "Intrapreneuring and Entrepreneuring: Myth or Reality for the Information Professional?" Continuing education and professional development courses carry titles such as "Making Money: Fees for Information Service," "How to Make Money Doing Research with Your Microcomputer," and "The Ins and Outs of Information Brokering." Those who charge fees fly to consult with those who might so do. Those adamant for free-to-all information rights write blistering editorial letters shaming librarians who would deny access to anyone at all.

The concept of "intrapreneuring"—of creating a business within a business—caught the imagination of virtually all segments of the business world in the mid-1980s. As one business school professor put it: "Entrepreneurs start businesses; corporate entrepreneurs, often called intrapreneurs, improve existing ones. In the same way that an entrepreneur comes up with an innovative idea and builds a company around

1

it, intrapreneurs come up with new ideas and implement them within their companies."[1]

Intrapreneurism in business was said to be "the key to survival in the 1980s." "Intrapreneurs help big firms think small." Intrapreneurs were called the "genius within," the "new business mavericks," "the new stars." Intrapreneurs were touted as the "new hope for new business," and the "favorite weapon of corporate strategists."[2]

The business press busied itself explaining how to start a small business inside a big one by "setting up entrepreneurial units," and how to "find room for the entrepreneur." Managers in all disciplines were given instructions on "the care and feeding of intrapreneurs," those "people with ideas."

Journalists seemed to enjoy the topic, producing articles with titles such as "What's in Among the Megatrendy," "Now Intrapreneurship Is Hot," "Intrapreneur—The New Buzzword," and "Business Fads: What's In—and Out."

FEE VS. FREE: CONSCIENTIOUS LIBRARIANS' DILEMMA

Traditional librarians—by nature, by training and by instinct—defend the premise that free access to information is essential. Free access to information is the backbone of a free society. Society pools its money, via taxes, so information can be gathered together on its behalf. Free access to the information that has been gathered is the right and privilege of all free people.

It would seem straightforward, then, that to charge a fee for access to information erects a barrier to free access and thereby works counter to goals for a free society. By tradition, fees are not ethical.

That information has value is not the debate and never has been the debate: timely, correct information has always been crucial. In 1775, Massachusetts colonial rebels vied with British royalists as each tried to get its own timely, correct version of Lexington/Concord happenings back to London before the other—everyone knew that the first information to arrive at court would carry most clout. Over 200 years later, the value of timely information and the value of professionals who arrange information so people can use it remain undisputed.[3]

Now new circumstances challenge old ethics and responsible librarians everywhere struggle to devise practical ways to cope.

From the agrarian economy of 1775, our society has changed so that today our biggest industry is information: more money now moves through our economy in pursuit of information-related activity than in pursuit of any other activity ("information" being, admittedly, very broadly defined). No longer is information confined in three-dimensional packages bought for finite prices. Today much information is available most quickly, and therefore most usefully, at pay-as-you-go prices. Some information is available no other way.

Librarians have weathered other information-packaging changes throughout the years without serious compromise of ethical free-to-all principles. Librarians buy and provide access to multiple types of information packages. Since no library can have everything anyone might want, libraries share resources with other libraries. In theory and in practice, people everywhere are served reasonably equally—although, since resource sharing can be clumsy, some wait longer than others to be served.

Pay-as-you-go services in libraries are, of course, not in themselves new. Most libraries provide access to the information-communicator called the telephone: patrons pay cash on the spot for using this information tool to suit individual needs. Most libraries provide access to information-copiers: patrons pay cash on the spot in amounts appropriate to immediate individual copying needs. With few exceptions, patrons know how to use telephones and copy machines, or can learn how with minimal help from library staff.

How to handle pay-as-you-go access to online databases, however, has created new challenges. First, most library patrons do not know how to access online databases: is the librarian to take time to do the search for the patron who doesn't know how? Is self-service online searching practical, even if the patron knows how, or claims to know how? Second: the learning curve, for those who wish to learn, is long: is the librarian to take time not only to learn how, but to become a teacher? Third: accessing most commercial online databases still costs exponentially more than using telephones or copy machines. No matter who does the searching, who is to pay communications charges and charges levied by commercial online vendors? The library? The patron? Databases on CD-ROM solve part of the problem: a CD-ROM database is bought by the library for a finite price and can be searched by library patrons at will at no additional cost. But who pays for access to information that changes daily, hourly—information not yet on a CD-ROM?

Librarians everywhere are struggling to keep up and to cope, practically, financially, and ethically. As one library administrator bemoans, "The clear lines between professionalism and commercialism have become blurred and will become still more unclear. . . .."[4]

SHOULD WE OR SHOULDN'T WE?

Whether or not to charge fees may well not be an obvious decision. Library directors and boards of trustees struggle with the issue, consultants are hired, reports are prepared. Public libraries, especially those in larger communities, feel political pressure from their municipalities to demonstrate that vigorous consideration has been given to increasing nontax revenues. Charging fees for selected services may seem a logical companion to other money-raising or money-saving tactics, and yet, as one library director asked, "Are we shooting ourselves in the foot by acting as if we didn't *need* public moneys?" State agencies that monitor and support public libraries are under pressure to supply whether-to and how-to guidelines.[5] News comes from sister libraries that "Britain's 5,000 public libraries could more than double their gross income by charging fees and contracting out services."[6]

For many, many librarians—and not only public librarians—the decision to avoid charging fees is obvious. There are other librarians for whom charging fees is almost a mandate. And, of course, there are myriad libraries in between with ambivalent let's-try-it-and-see policies. One library director, when queried on fee-based service in his library, confessed that "deciding whether or not it should be done" was far and away more difficult than any other aspect of fee-based services.

Once a decision to charge service fees in some manner or other is made by whomever the decisionmaker happens to be, attitudes of librarians involved in day-to-day transactions run the gamut. Some are highly uncomfortable in the new role. Typical complaint: "They're making us librarians count beans." "This is the first time in a long library career where I have had to institute charges, and making sure that I am fair to all has been the hardest part," says one librarian, who is echoed by another who says "I really hate the library functioning around having to make money." An academic librarian says, "One of the most difficult aspects of being involved in a fee-based service here has been fighting the traditional philosophy of free library service. We anticipated resistance and believe me, we've got it."

Some objections are very personal, such as for the individual who "still would like not to charge those nursing students who are my personal friends," and another who "knows people who could benefit from the service but they can't afford it."

Some wish they could turn back the clock and start differently. Typical: "We probably should have charged for workshops and training from the beginning—we failed to convince management that we can't start charging for what we've been giving away free for years." One librarian feels that fee-charging came about by coercion: "Because the state of XXX has given me the same budget for five years, I had to begin charging for searches and photocopies last summer. The last year has meant working out the problems and complaints of charging for items that used to be 'free.'" Another state librarian says, "The climate of opinion here has a great deal to do with how successful fee charging will be—the public is completely unaware of the costs of information retrieval, and we should have done more broadside education before starting with fees." A senior university librarian thinks that "the context for the service should have been addressed before we began. It goes beyond institutional goals and reaches into institutional culture and politics."

Some librarians report that fee-based service has made life infinitely easier. For instance, occasionally academic libraries inherit vaguely affiliated patrons whose access privileges were bestowed much as informal knighthoods, or who are "sponsored" by a senior faculty member or department head. As one librarian happily managing a fee-based service confesses, "Formerly it was necessary to—I hate to say it—trust the sponsor's integrity. Our new program offers an option and no longer makes it necessary to 'stretch the truth,' as sometimes happened." Another librarian, this one in a medical school, agrees: "This hasn't been hard, it's been easy. It used to be harder to turn away nonaffiliated persons with genuine need when we didn't have the ability to provide options for them."[7]

WHO SELLS WHAT, TO WHOM, FOR HOW MUCH?

Fee-based services exist in academic libraries, in public libraries, in medical libraries. Associations sell fee-based information services. Special libraries charge back, which is "selling" to insiders, and charge out, which is selling to outside customers of the parent institution. In supplying fee-based information services, librarians find themselves in a competitive market place: also selling information service are research and development firms, independent information entrepreneurs, professional societies, database vendors, government agencies,[8] publishers, media services, and more.[9]

Librarians offering fee-based services hold a wealth of titles: agency head, business science technology reference librarian, business searcher, business information specialist, campus delivery specialist, chair of computer search department, circuit librarian, coordinator of fee-based project, database librarian, full-time reference librarian with searching and teaching duties, information center head, information delivery librarian, marketing services manager, photograph archivist, reference librarian, research manager, scientific network manager, technical information service specialist, etc.

These people are expected to be paragons. A recent "Notice of Vacancy" at an eastern university required "extensive experience in the use of scientific, technical, or business data/information sources, preferably in a corporate or technical setting. Graduate degree in one of the sciences, or a business-related area," plus an MLS. This person was to have "excellent communication and interpersonal skills to build a continuing base of support for the program within the university, as well as to undertake an aggressive external marketing effort." Among responsibilities were "marketing, advertising, and delivery of information services to businesses, associations, agencies, entrepreneurs, and other nonuniversity users of data in the state."

The list of what services are currently being sold by libraries is equally varied. Among those so far reported:

- access to library collections through online catalog
- access to library database, both hardcopy and online
- assistance to researchers (usually authors)
- bibliographic citations
- book loans from the collection
- borrowing privileges
- cataloging
- citation clarification
- commodity reports
- computer database searching education
- computerized search services
- consulting services
- country profiles
- credit reports
- current awareness bulletins
- current awareness lists

- document delivery
- electronic mail
- evaluative review of literature (a value-added function)
- general information
- InfoDash (staff "dashers" are sent to retrieve documents)
- interlibrary loan
- literature searching
- long-distance phone calls
- market research
- microfiching for people going overseas
- obtaining requested materials
- orientation
- photocopy service
- pull services (items available at desk for quick pickup)
- reprints
- research
- retrospective topical bibliographies
- selective dissemination of information (SDIs)
- taking opinion polls on the telephone
- telefacsimile services[10]
- training event notices
- translations
- Walk-in-Library service (providing work space)

As one librarian put it, "We try to get anything for anybody who purchases a membership card."

Instead of or in addition to selling information-related *services*, some libraries are selling information-linked *products*—conference proceedings, how-we-did-it-good guidelines, outreach program details, etc. At least one large public library, through its Friends group, sends out a mail order gift catalog of book-related gifts such as special editions of children's classics, reproductions of antique woodcuts, puzzles, literary games. Several libraries sell to other libraries software developed for their own use (from catalog card creation to streamlining interlibrary loan).

Librarians reporting on their fee-based activities count practically every kind of client among their customers. A sampling:

- ad agencies
- allied health personnel
- alumni
- biomedical businesses
- business managers
- consultants
- corporations
- faculty from small colleges
- Fortune 500 companies
- freelance engineers
- government (all levels, and not limited to the U.S.)
- hospitals
- individuals with health/medical information needs
- industry of various sizes
- information brokers
- lawyers
- nurses, nursing homes
- oil well people in the field
- physicians
- public relations firms
- publishers
- small business community
- state agency personnel
- students from colleges and universities
- testing laboratories

As one librarian put it, "We sell to anyone regardless of affiliation."

How many requests per year does a fee-based service receive? What is the volume of business? There is no average, no typical reply to these questions. The smallest services fill perhaps one request a week and the largest will fill 600 in the same period.

Presumably the dollar volume spread is equally wide, although exact figures are hard to come by: "Our dollar volume is not really publishable" is a typical response. One rather unhappy-sounding librarian says, "Our volume is steady at present, but less than it needs to be to recover cost."

How much do fee-based services charge? Mention an

amount, and someone is charging it. Librarians share a good deal of discomfort about rate setting,[11] which either takes the form of trying to find out what other library fee-based services are charging, or comparing (usually unfavorably) proposed fees to one's own take-home salary.

Most librarians seem to feel they must figure out what to charge all by themselves, rather than seek help from the controllers office, or the treasurer, or the financial officer. Many librarians feel that fees, once set, turn out to have been set too low. Some fee structures seem ungainly or overcomplicated while others are haphazard: "I am concerned that we are charging too little. We don't have a good idea of what the service is costing us since it is run out of one of my desk drawers. . . ."

THE STRESS FACTOR

Being a librarian in a fee-based service can be exhilarating, exciting, energizing. And yet there is virtually always pressure and stress. As one fee-based veteran points out, "Most librarians have little or no fiscal or marketing training for developing such services, and there are very few opportunities for self-education in this field. Some librarians are *forced* into this role by higher ups."

The job is often lonely. Librarians doing the job can be misunderstood and mistrusted by colleagues. Many, if not most, fee-based librarians have to grow in their jobs and develop their services virtually by themselves. All they can do is their best, and they are.

Typical: "Hardest is the frustration of never breaking even—given the problems of running a 'business' within an academic (i.e., bureaucratic) setting—always being under the gun—never getting much of a salary increase because the income generated is not enough. The administration seems unaware of our problems." Another confesses, "When I do need assistance from management (marketing), they leave it all to me. When I *don't* need their help (fee-setting), they thrust it on me." Yet another: "It's hard dealing with the fast pace and stress that never lets up. There is also a sense of isolation at first—others don't really understand what you are doing. Most other librarians here don't see the time-equals-money correlation, and haven't fathomed that if I don't use my time wisely, I'll no longer have a job."

One librarian says, "I offered the service to local special librarians at a party we were all at. They were polite, but they have since boycotted our service." And a sad confession: "Hardest is explaining to my friends what I am doing!"

References

1. Rosabeth Moss Kanter, "How to be an entrepreneur without leaving your company," *Working Woman*, November 1988, p. 44.
2. These and the following short quotations are from a multi-database online search at a Bibliographic Retrieval Service (BRS) sales demonstration in Anaheim, California, in June 1987.
3. See especially *President's Task Force on the Value of the Information Professional*, a report to the Special Libraries Association (SLA) 1987 annual meeting. Copies of the final report are available from SLA, 1700 18th St., NW, Washington, DC 20009.
4. Quotation from James F. Govan, "The creeping invisible hand: entrepreneurial librarianship," *Library Journal*, January 1988, pp. 35-38. The author points out that today's librarians are under pressure to produce revenues. "The last 20 years have witnessed a *crise de conscience* that began with photocopying and flourishes today over online searching. [There is] an entirely different atmosphere for librarians, one in which fees for service—once regarded with the same reprehension as a doctor's ad—not only becomes acceptable, but in which income replaces satisfied patrons as the overriding goal."

- See also Sheila S. Intner & Jorge R. Schement, "The ethic of free service," *Library Journal*, 1 October 1987, pp. 50-52. The article is a thoughtful discussion which "raises questions about library ethos toward information: freely shared resource or commodity for sale?" About online computer services: "Can this new brand of high-tech information find happiness in an environment where information is believed to be a free public

good? The authors point out that, in our burgeoning information economy, librarians find their profession in the limelight:
"The irony of this development is that it has not brought
harmony to the profession. Instead, it has brought conflict. It is
possible that the field [librarianship] will split between professional information technocrats and librarians . . ."

- Local papers carry articles such as "Growing fees at public
  libraries spur concern for the 'information poor,'" *Ann Arbor*
  (Michigan) *News* (16 September 1987, via the Associated Press)
  which discusses the difference between provision of 'basic
  services' and 'extensive personal services.'

  Even parking fees which limit parking time and copy machine charges higher than those at other library copy machines
  are triggering furor. See A.J. Anderson's "How do you manage?" column "The money-making library," *Library Journal*, 15
  September 1987, pp. 57-59.

  Editorial opinions on fees are believable, persuasive, and
  can be adamant. Examples: John Berry's "Practice and principle: the fee example" (*Library Journal*, 1 February 1988, p. 4)
  and "Putting principle above 'research'" (*Library Journal*, 15
  June 1988, p. 4).

  Typical of letters to the editor is "No fees for anything" from
  a public library director to *Library Journal* (15 April 1988, p. 6)
  which avers that "there is no place in the operation of a modern
  public library for the imposition of fees for access to any library
  material."

- A book on fee ethics and fee decision-making in public libraries
  is: Pete Giacoma, *The Fee or Free Decision: Legal, Economic,
  Political, and Ethical Perspectives for Public Libraries*, Neal-
  Schuman Publishers, 1989. From the foreword by Gerald R.
  Shields: "This book is the ammunition you need. . . . When you
  finish this book, you will find that you have absorbed a reasoned and dispassionate manifesto. . . ." Puts fee-charging in
  historical and political perspective. An in-depth study, many
  references and notes.

- General analyses of information service fees, both by Alice
  Sizer Warner, are: "Fees for information service" in *The Information Profession: Facing Future Challenges*, proceedings of
  1987 Special Libraries Association State-of-the-Art Institute,
  pp. 73-85; and "Fees for service: state of the art" in *Wilson
  Library Bulletin*, April 1989, pp. 55-57 (adapted from a lecture

at the 1988 Alberta L. Brown Lecture Series at Western
Michigan University, Kalamazoo).

5. An example is the study commissioned in 1987-88 by the
   Commonwealth of Pennsylvania to examine the role of fees in
   public libraries. In response to pressures on librarians and
   trustees to consider fees because of rising costs, the Advisory
   Council on Library Development of the State Library was asked
   to produce guidelines. After a year, it was reported to me by
   telephone that "the Council decided that fees were not significant and therefore not an issue." Information from the Office of
   the Library Development Director, State Library of Pennsylvania, Box 1601, Harrisburg PA 17105.
6. Cited in *Library Hotline*, 14 March 1988, p. 3, from a Green Paper
   published by Britain's Arts Minister, "Financing Our Public
   Library Service: Four Subjects for Debate: A Consultative Paper," CM 324, HMSO.
7. Discussion of fee-based services in libraries may be found in
   issues of the bi-monthly newsletter, *Information Broker* (formerly *The Journal of Fee-Based Information Services*) published by
   Burwell Enterprises, 5106 FM 1960 W. #349, Houston, TX
   77069. Also the substantial collection of articles in: Robin Kinder
   and Bill Katz, eds., *Information Brokers and Reference Services*,
   Haworth Press, 1988 (also published as No. 29 of the journal, *The
   Reference Librarian*).
8. Among long-time government fee-based online search services
   are installations in various parts of the United States sponsored
   by the National Aeronautic and Space Administration. The
   director of one of these writes: "We sell computerized search
   services to industrial clients with the aim of increasing American
   industrial competitiveness. We are congressionally mandated to
   do this, and receive NASA support." In many regions, the U.S.
   Department of Commerce offers access to online databases to
   American businesses.
9. There is no single comprehensive listing of *all* suppliers of fee-
   based information services. Suggested sources:

   • *Directory of Fee-Based Information Services,* published annu-
     ally by Burwell Enterprises, 5106 FM 1960 W., #349, Hous-
     ton, TX 77069. Lists both information entrepreneurs and
     intrapreneurships. Probably the most complete listing available.

- "Dialorder suppliers," a listing of document delivery sources from which document copies may be ordered online via Dialog Information Services, Inc., is part of the user-manual documentation provided by Dialog to online-searching customers. The same information is available online. Dialog Information Services, Inc., 3460 Hillview Ave., Palo Alto, CA 94304.
- A more complete listing of document delivery sources is *Document Retrieval Sources and Service,* published by and available from The Information Store, 140 2nd St., San Francisco, CA 94105.
- FISCAL (Fee-Based Information Service Centers in Academic Libraries) has been organized within the American Library Association. For information on current membership lists contact ALA, 50 E. Huron St., Chicago, IL 60611.

10. See "A city/county library tries intra-faxing," *American Libraries,* January 1988, pp. 62-63.
11. See "How will fees be set?" later in this book, in Chapter Three, *Planning.*

____2____
Activity

FEE-BASED SERVICES IN ACADEMIC LIBRARIES

Most academic libraries offer online searching for students and faculty at little more than out-of-pocket cost. However, many (no one is sure of the exact number) academic libraries have also established fee-based services for customers outside the academic community. The services commonly offered are online and manual research, photocopying articles and other documents, and book loans from the library's collections.

In theory, the how-to's of charging for information services reflect both the financial and social goals of the institution from which the services come. Although the fees themselves vary widely, nonaffiliates are virtually invariably charged more than are students and faculty. A university may have as a social goal for a fee-based service that of maintaining good town-gown relationships: the fee-based service allows nonaffiliated people to use the library, and this is good public relations. A university may also use its fee-based service as a way to keep alumni—especially rich alumni—in contact with the university: fund raisers know that keeping in steady contact with potential donors is always a smart move. Financial goals are based on various levels of cost recovery, and there are as many interpretations of exactly what costs should be counted as recoverable as there are academic libraries offering fee-based services.[1]

Stories of how fee-based services developed and of the librarians who started them show that virtually every service essentially invented itself, and that the head librarians of these services have had to design their own management mechanisms and develop professionally in virtual isolation: they became "old hands" the hard way.

An example: "In December 1980 I left the security of the reference department of the graduate library at XYZ University and created a fee-based service—knowing that if I was not successful I would be out of a job. My interest was, to say the least, very high in making sure that I could create a fee-based service that would truly recover all costs. Since then, we've been given ILL to run and we've started a campus delivery service for faculty: they tell us what books and articles they want and we get them from libraries on campus and deliver them to their offices. We charge back to their university accounts at [so-and-so-much] . . . a page."

From another: "When we started way back when, in those days when there wasn't any online anything, we got 539 requests the first year. Now we get 40 or 50 times that." Another: "We have provided fee-based services to industry for more than 20 years. Until recently, services were document delivery and literature searching. Now we're trying to broaden the scope to include problem solving, information synthesis, and analysis."

Yet another: "Since 1974 when I wrote my masters degree paper on 'The Independent Information Specialist,' I have been urging libraries to charge money for *service* connected with information delivery as opposed to the concept of a client using library facilities without extra help. If he/she could do computer searches him/herself, then pay the computer charges and that would be just. If assistance is needed, it should be paid for. Anyway, I've finally gotten to be coordinator of a state-wide service based in our state university library, so I'm getting a chance to put my ideas to the test."

The supply of service-starters continues. "I am coordinator of ABC, a fee-based service which was created to serve the nonuniversity community in the central part of the state. The service is still fairly new and in the evaluation stage." Another: "As database librarian here at the university for nine years, I recently established a fee-based service to fill information needs of the academic community as well as those of the the business and professional community."

Yet another: "We started this service because we are the only public university in this part of the state. There is no local private information broker, and there are lots of high tech firms: we were getting constant demands at the reference desk for access to articles through ILL and for other services. We just *had* to start charging fees. I did all practical planning and implementation in a three-month period, including Christmas."

One fee-based service, in a state university, has a contract with a major manufacturing company to be their stand-by, library research arm. And yet another report of a startup: "My connection is that I was qualified with an MBA and had a number of years serving in the business and government through active participation in the Chamber of Commerce, attendance at County Commissioner meetings, etc. I 'volunteered' to help QRS [a private university] set up its fee-based service, and as of September, here I've been!"

Several fee-based services are grappling with problems of attitude and perception. Says one: "The conservative nature of the university inhibits entrepreneurial efforts. There is no interest in our offering service which does not fit into the already existing workflow." Others report that professors fear that the book they themselves might want to use today will be unavailable, "rented" to a fee-based customer, an "outsider."

The largest, oldest university fee-based-service-to-outsiders services are, as of this writing, fielding about 20,000 requests a year: 120 requests each business day, almost 15 requests an hour with a new request every four minutes (were requests to be evenly spaced, which of course they never are). "The smallest job can be copying an article for just a few dollars, the largest can be in the thousands of dollars," says one of the veteran librarians.

A ten-year-old university fee-based service reports 149 literature searches, 6,442 document delivery requests, and some 400 customers served in a recent fiscal year. Another university service says, "In seven years we have served 2,700 +

companies and 700+ individuals." One of the newer services reports 400 to 500 transactions a month, with most document delivery activity in the engineering field. Several other academic librarians report that they do about 1,000 searches per year. The smallest, low-key services have one or two customers a week. Staff size, of course, varies as well. Some services use one or two people, others employ dozens when support staff are counted.

Some larger universities have more than one fee-based service on campus. One quasi-public university has three fee-based services in three specialty-school libraries. Each charges wildly differing rates: $25, $55, and $90 an hour. Each head librarian feels the service's price is reasonable, defensible, and collectable.

A few universities charge nonaffiliates for membership, perhaps $1,000 to $3,000 or more a year, and have two fee scales: a low one for nonaffiliate members, who get priority service, and a high scale for nonaffiliate nonmembers, who must wait their turn. At one university the members pay $50 an hour, nonmembers pay $80. At another, clients can become members and, as members, get priority service and a 20 percent discount. Charges, in this case, are figured according to a deceptively simple-sounding formula based on a multiplier, the number of minutes recorded at the end of an online search, and out-of-pocket costs.

Prices vary around the country. At a branch of a southern state university, computer search services are billed out at $24 an hour plus direct costs: a one-hour minimum, then quarter-hour increments. An eastern urban university charges $20 per half hour for staff time with a one-hour minimum. At a New England university, university affiliates (faculty and students) are billed out-of-pocket costs for online searching, plus 50 percent of the out-of-pocket costs. Nonaffiliated outsiders pay the same plus $60 an hour, with a one-hour minimum. A midwestern university is "searching applicable databases . . . for $40 per hour plus toll calls, computer charges, and shipping."

It is reported that at a west coast university 20 of their libraries will search (in their respective fields) for a $20 search fee plus costs—by appointment only. Another western university charges $50 an hour for searching, with an added wrinkle: "Copies of government microfiche are charged to all patrons at a lower rate if they pick them up personally."

Prices at some universities seem, at first glance, to be unduly complicated. At one university there are *ten* categories of fees payers (Membership Card, Alumni, Retired Staff, VIP Members, etc.) with as many variations of charges and discounts for various services.

Presumably prices are set with specific cost recovery goals in mind. One university charges $70 an hour, and librarians are expected to bill at least 2.5 hours per day as contribution to total cost recovery (heat, light, university overhead) of the fee-based division. Another fee-based service bases its charges around a goal of recovering salaries and benefits, "but not space and electricity." Yet another fee-based service had as a goal to clear (a precise definition of "clear" was not available) $45,000 in its first year; in actuality, they cleared $38,000. Several librarians shoot for finite monthly amounts, such as $5,000 or $9,000; again, it is hard to tell whether these amounts represent the total volume of business or the total "profit." Some fees seem less than logical. One university fee-based service charges $60 an hour and the librarian doesn't know how that price was arrived at—he inherited it.

In a rare moment of candor, one fee-based service librarian shared how her budget breaks down and what elements must be considered in planning for cost recovery—all of which determines how fees are set.

Approximately 41 percent of the budget is used for classified and unclassified salaries and student wages. University policy requires adding an additional 29 percent to salaries to help defray costs for such fringe benefits as vacations, sick leave, and medical insurance. The staff is made up of myself, full-time, a three-quarter time reference librarian, a full-time clerk, a one-third time fiscal clerk and the equivalent of 80 hours per week in student help. . . . Approximately 55 percent of our budget is spent on supplies and services. This is a broad category that includes a wide spectrum of supplies for the operation of an efficient labor-intensive office. . . . The remaining 4 percent of our budget is set aside for new capital equipment, replacements or repairs.[2]

With only a few exceptions, there is little how-to material available about setting up a fee-based service in an academic library. Much of what is available is more philosophical than practical. Most fee-based librarian support groups are informal and unadvertised. The older, more established fee-based service librarians are getting tired of being asked to tell others how to set up a fee-based service. Typical is a letter received when research was being carried out for this book: "Since we receive so many requests like yours, we have decided to offer our services as consultants, the fee to be determined on an individual basis." Most established fee-based service librarians agree that pressures are such that fellow and sister librarians should take their place as fee payers when seeking how-to-start information.

FEE-BASED SERVICES IN PUBLIC LIBRARIES[3]

Public library fees are an extremely hot political topic not only in the United States, but in much of the world. The Working Group on Charges of the International Federation of Library Associations (IFLA) has drawn comparisons between countries with "free" (i.e., tax-supported) public library services and other countries where a charge is made for some services. Advantages of charging fees are found to be few. The Working Group "considered that certain ideals and standards were basic to the public library service and that any barrier to books or other materials would lead, almost certainly, to a decline in library use." The group at large voted unanimously to "re-affirm the concept of public library service freely available for borrowing and consultation of library materials."[4]

Some public librarians, rejecting, as does IFLA, fee-charging, consider obvious alternatives: increasing revenues at the institutional level, increasing efficiency of existing resources, restructuring service priorities, or reallocating existing resources.[5] Imposing obviously visible limitations on services to patrons (such as closing doors all day on Saturdays) has been known to cause enough hue and cry to divert extra funds to the library. Many—probably most—public librarians have simply avoided offering online searching service so as to avoid having to grapple with the practicalities and emotions of fee charging.

The development of databases on CD-ROM is not only an exciting technical development, it appears to be a solution to a moral dilemma as well: patrons can search a database on CD-ROM at will, at "no additional cost to anyone," therefore causing no headaches or agony over issues of fees vs. free access. The problem, however, is that CD-ROMs are at the moment very expensive; libraries somehow have to absorb their cost.

In spite of, and in the face of, controversy, increasing numbers of U.S. public librarians are offering fee-based research services. For instance, one librarian says: "I came here [medium-sized mid-western city] with an idea for a fee-based service. The idea was accepted, and I began the new service in January 1986." At another library, librarians in the business, science and technology department already use online services at their own discretion in fielding "free" reference questions. "The only time a fee is charged for information here is if an online search is specifically requested—the fee is collected from the patron when the search is made. About five to six searches are done per month. We do not publicize the service."

Another librarian says, "I am agency head for the new XYZ Research Center [in an industrial city]. My primary responsibility is to aggressively market this new service, but we all know that before one can market, one must plan. So I have just completed the Center's business plan." A handful of public libraries have had fee-based departments for over 15 years: fee-based service as an alternative to help-yourself service is simply taken for granted.

Hourly charges vary hugely—$15 to $85 an hour at last count—and it seems that geographic location is not a factor. Some services reevaluate and increase prices regularly, others stay the same: at least one service charged $25 an hour for at least five years in a row.

A few libraries charge one rate for support service, and a higher rate for a librarian's time. Those that do have such billing rate gradations recommend against it: to explain rates to clients is awkward and record keeping can get clumsy. At least one library uses ". . . the ten-ten-ten rule, where the first ten minutes are paid for by the library, the second ten minutes by the patron, the third ten minutes by the library, and any additional minutes by the patron."[6]

Some libraries' fees are set in agreement with others: patent searches are offered in the science department of a large metropolitan library for $30 an hour, "because that's what others in the consortium charge."

At a west coast public library, "patron pays costs only, there are no search fees; patron comes by appointment and some groundwork must have been done." Another large metropolitan library charges "$15 per hour for staff time and overhead plus the cost of the search, including online, communication, and print charges. We also charge a flat fee for company searches and for market share searches, and we have to be sure the patron understands that the charge applies whether we find what she's looking for or not." (One librarian feels that this last situation, that of charging a fee whether or not an answer is found, is ". . . a problem with our profession. Doctors submit a bill," she says, "even if they can't diagnose the illness—and lawyers bill even if they lose the case.")

Goals of fee-based services in public libraries vary much as do prices, yet goals statements are harder to come by than are price lists. The financial goal of one of the older public library fee-based services is to recover the salaries of three people plus benefits (35% of salary) but not to recover cost of physical space, which in its case is about 750 square feet. The library's billing rate is $60 an hour, and billing is figured in 15-minute increments.

FEES CHARGED BY SPECIALIZED LIBRARIES

Some for-profit companies house libraries with their own customers—customers who may or may not be buyers of the companies' primary services. How fees are set and collected and accounted for differs from company to company; details are virtually always confidential.

An example of special libraries with customers of their own: accountants who leave large accounting companies to go out on their own often, as company "graduates," are allowed to continue to use the services of the alma mater company's library—for a fee. Similar arrangements with varying degrees of formality are seen in law firms, research and development firms, etc.

Another example: several significant company clients of a large aeronautics company had been deeply impressed by the caliber of the company's Information Center and of its librarians' services. More as a public relations move than anything else, the aeronautics company president told his clients to feel free to ask any question, any time—the librarians would be glad to help. One thing led to another; the number of questions multiplied, the questions became complex and turned into projects, and the Information Center found itself—with everyones' blessing—charging fees to its own customers.

Another example is the one-person library in a small contract research firm. Buoyed by comments from one of their clients who said, "Boy! I sure could use some help like that," the librarian suggested to her firm's president that the library might experiment with providing services for clients outside the firm—start a business within a business, an intrapreneurship. Her arguments were persuasive. It would bring greater visibility for the firm and it would produce income. As one observer of this intrapreneurship wrote, ". . . corporate and business librarians have long recognized that providing library and information services for the parent company is a corporate expense. But if the information center is bringing in money, it becomes a profit center."[7] Extra work generated on behalf of outside clients was accomplished with the help of hourly, part-time librarians. This experimental intrapreneurship, successful in itself, was terminated a couple of years later when the librarian departed to start her own entrepreneurial information venture.

Another special library that charges fees directly to customers is a newspaper library, which has "installed a research charge for assisting researchers (usually authors) in obtaining necessary materials." Yet another example is reported by a self-employed librarian: "As an expert independent consultant, I was asked by a major U.S. corporation to design and organize a photographic/slide collection and library. While the library is used mainly for public relations purposes, the uniqueness and value of the photographic images suggested a strong case for charging for their use to offset cost of reproduction and wear and tear on the collection."

FEES CHARGED BY MEDICAL LIBRARIES[8]

Many health care libraries have variations and combinations of access fees, cost reimbursement fees, and/or service fees. Many facilities without fee structures are exploring options. Typical: "I am in charge of instituting a fee-for-service system for our medical college library; we've been charging for interlibrary loans and computer searches and cataloging services already, and we need new prices and publicity." Another: "We are a hospital-based library service that is developing a fee-for-service proposal; we are trying *not* to charge back to departments that do not have an external source of funding (grants, etc.), so we want *outside* money coming in."

At least one librarian is encountering difficulties in justifying fee-charging to hospital management. "They keep asking how they, a nonprofit institution, can have a fee-based inhouse service because they can't figure out how to determine the profit they're not making. For instance, they can't rent space. They can't offer nonhealth-related courses. So how can I charge fees? Their lawyers are checking into it, which is where *I* should have checked in the first place."[9]

One medical college librarian says, "Our program provides fee-for-service access to nonaffiliated health professionals. At the present time, the library does no copying, even for primary clientele—services are 'access only.' Online literature searches are sold to outsiders, free to medical students." Access fees are $2,000 a year for profit-making institutions, and $1,000 a year for nonprofit institutions: the fee buys one card in the name of whomever the subscriber specifies and extra cards cost extra ($200 and $100). Individual health professionals may have access to this library for $300 a year.

An academic medical center library facility supporting multiple institutions bills these institutions as well as outsiders (law firms, private corporations, individuals, etc.) for services: database searching, document delivery (over 40,000 per year), etc.

The library at a state medical center uses online databases to answer reference questions, entirely at the discretion of the reference librarian. There is no charge to the patron. In the same library, and at the same reference desk, Online Search Service (for a fee) produces a product: a printout. After experimentation, the librarian decided to charge a flat fee for this service. Advantages for the patron are that the patron knows exactly what the search is going to cost and can easily authorize searches on the spot. Advantages for the library are that the fee structure is easy to learn and to explain, bills are simple to calculate and can be made out on the spot, and things (i.e., expensive vs. inexpensive searches) even out in the long run.[10]

A small community hospital reports that it does not charge anything to its "immediate user group." Thirty percent are staff physicians who donate "a percentage of their dues" to the library; 30 percent are hospital administrators; 30 percent are student nurses who, the librarian says, "are not expensive to serve. They do pay for their own photocopying. And if the nurses need searches done for reasons outside the hospital (such as they are getting their bachelor's degrees at a local college or university), then they are charged by the hospital for those searches. If anyone is going to give them free searches, it ought to be the library at the college or university."

The final 10 percent of this library's users are "billed for online charges, for copying charges, and $20 an hour for time." These users include "hospitals with no online capability and some patients. Public libraries send some customers, after careful screening." Of this 10 percent, the librarian says: "We have been discouraging them and are sending them to freelancers. We could make several thousand dollars a year, between the copy machine and selling searches, but since this money doesn't go into the library budget, it kinds of removes the incentive. We do keep track, though, and use the figures as weapons when budget cuts are threatened."

A library in a critical care hospital in a metropolitan suburb has a policy of charging outsiders a flat fee for online medical searches: $40 per search, with search results downloaded into and printed off of the library's personal computer. At the request of the board of trustees, the library does not advertise this capability, yet stands ready to respond to requests from those in need.

Another library, this one at a leading university medical school, has a layered list of modest charges. For a "mini-search" on one out of four medical databases, it will print online 50 citations without abstracts or 25 citations with abstracts for a flat fee of $20.00 for university affiliates and $27.50 for outsiders. Comprehensive searches are by appointment only. The librarian reserves one and a half hours to work on strategy with the client, who sits with the librarian at the computer. Costs vary and can include online costs, offline printing costs, a $7.50 handling charge, and a $25 surcharge for nonaffiliates.

Other fee structures seem ungainly and over-complicated, as in this example from a hospital library: "Fees are charged to the medical staff for searches, ILLs, and copies. Fees are charged to the public for the same services, but at a higher rate. No fees or charge back system for the hospital staff or medical staff are lower than for public, but higher than for medical staff needing patient care information. Medical staff fees recover direct variable costs. Personal use fees for hospital and medical staff recover both direct fixed and variable costs. Public use fees recover both and direct fixed and indirect fixed and variable costs." A complicated system indeed for what turns out to be "a small volume hospital—five searches a month, ten ILLs, eight 'mediated' copies and 32 self-serve in coin op."

One hospital librarian, using hospital computer facilities, has developed an information product: software which, in conjunction with telefacsimile, speeds up interlibrary loan and makes the whole process less labor intensive. The hospital holds rights to the software it sells, the librarian divides her time between the library and the software project.[11]

FEES CHARGED BY ASSOCIATION LIBRARIES

By and large, association librarians have an especially hard time struggling with fees. The association librarian typically works alone, doing everything from opening mail to fielding telephone calls—and lone librarians, while they revel in lack of supervision, need guidance and colleagial support when setting fees. Says one senior librarian, "Association librarians need all the bolstering they can get—*that* is a tough row to hoe!" There is at least one ad hoc group of association librarians that meets for brown bag lunches to discuss mutual fee problems.

Some associations do not charge at all for information services. An example: "Five years ago we got around 500 calls a month from members and nonmembers. We had 2,540 requests for information this past month, and so we now limit our services to members and for them everything is free. The copy machine is free, phone calls are free. The whole system seems to work, and our vice president has never said anything about cutting the budget. He feels the library is a good will gesture and that members have already paid for information services when they pay their dues. Our association has a legal group which keeps in close contact with the state associations; this legal advice is 'free' to members, too."

Not all librarians agree that their services should be free. Says one: "The only thing we sell is computer searches. We *give* everything else away (digests, bibliographies, information, etc.). All materials and staff time are free, and I think our members value us less because of it. We do training on a cost recovery basis—for that we charge transportation and a per diem, but that's all."

In general, those association libraries that do charge fees tend to charge to nonmembers at an exorbitant rate and to members at an affordable rate (definitions of "exorbitant" and "affordable" vary) with the goal being to convert nonmembers to membership. Beyond that, association librarians have worked out a variety of fee systems. At one association, for instance, the librarian reports: "We do not charge members unless it's a special research effort, and then we sell the staff's time and expertise to deliver a compilation of resources to provide the most appropriate answer(s). Our volume is small—five to ten requests a month that generate income."

Another says: "We are developing an information data-base specific to our field which will be available to our association members at a low price and to the public at higher cost. We 'sell' reprints of anything we have that is registered with the Copyright Clearance Center. We also have a rental library of 2,500 volumes." Yet another reports: "Two of us answer 700 to 800 queries per month, mostly from members. Anything we've had to pay for, like computer searches, is reimbursed to us, but our time is free."

At least one trade association information center has taken the step of making available to the public at large their database of unique information—for a fee. In 1980, requests from members for information were increasing. Library resources centered (typically) on vast clippings files and on close to 200 periodicals. The periodicals had been manually indexed since the late 1960s (admittedly not a typical situation). The information center director reports that, "on hot topics we had to pore through four to five folders two inches thick or in some cases on really hot topics one yard's worth of files. At that time there was no index to the type of materials we were dealing with. The obvious solution was to automate,"[12] which they did, starting with the periodicals file and moving through other materials in the Information Center. What started as a private file is now publicly available through well-known database vendors. Despite the database, the request volume at the library has not diminished as many members prefer personalized service rather than a high tech search.

CHARGING BACK

Charging back is a mechanism wherein services are charged back to departments, to projects, to jobs: the accounting department debits money from the appropriate department account, project account, or job account, and credits that money to the library's account.

There is great variety in how library charge backs are managed. It is common, but by no means universal, to charge back out-of-pocket costs, such as costs of doing an online search, to the individual or department ordering the search. Some libraries charge back for time encumbered by a search as well. Some libraries charge for cataloging: at least one university library charges academic departments for cataloging books in the departments' subject fields. Similar charge backs occur in special libraries.

A university example of charging back: "The reference department (*not* the fee-based service department) charges back literature searches to individuals (e.g., students) or departments (faculty) who pay on an interdepartmental charge form—there is a slight overhead on computer charges only." A university fee-based service reports that "charging back to departments is done through transfer vouchers (university paperwork), and fees (set by us) are approved by the Cost Reimbursement Office. We have no quotas, and have to keep our paperwork for seven years. We generate the paperwork and send the other university accounts a copy of the transfer voucher to match up when the charge appears on their university statement or account." When document copying at yet another university, "we use a VendaCard system on photocopy machines to keep track of number of copies—each department has its own card, kept in the library."

At one large university medical school library, medical librarians develop and maintain departmental collections. This service is charged back to the departments that have use of the collections at the annual rate of $9,700 per year for one day a week of a librarian's time, or $4,850 for half a day a week. This works out to about $25 an hour.

In another program, librarians provide informational back-up for Thursday morning medical case presentations. For this there is an annual charge of $4,400. This represents 364 hours of work a year, divided between librarians and support staff, for the various tasks; the average charge-back rate is $12.09 per hour.

Specific charge-back dollar rates at special libraries in for-profit institutions range widely; exact rates are confidential and rarely published. "We set our rates based upon budget expenditures allocated by product line with an estimate for demand," is a typical statement.

There is great variation in how special libraries manage charging back issues. One corporate library reports that it "... has a mandate to fully recover all costs, including salaries, benefits, out-of-pocket expenses, rent and utilities, and internal allocations." Another corporate information center with 22 full-time staffers "charges *all* of its costs back to users. All customers are internal. About 25 percent is charged back for individual services (searches, interlibrary loans, documents, translations, etc.) and 75 percent is charged back on a head-count basis as an annual 'access fee.' Our goal is to charge back 100% of costs to users, and we set our rates based on this cost recovery."

Many charge-back mechanisms run smoothly. A utility company librarian says, "We track all usage and send a sum-marized bill to the corporate system tracking charge backs in our entity. Bills by entity are then handled by the corporate accounts people—they keep track."

A librarian in a leading manufacturing company, "charges departments the direct costs incurred for document delivery and online searching—we do not charge for staff time. There is no challenge with the money, we simply pass on our costs. The charges are handled on books at central accounting; the library staff compiles monthly department charges, and sends the list to accounting. No money changes hands, and no bills are sent."

A headquarters librarian in a large conglomerate says, "we charge back to operating companies, but only for out-of-pockets. We get monthly bills from vendors and pay them. We use a log on our spreadsheet program to charge back quarterly to the operating companies for search and retrieval charges only—we send an interoffice memo to accounting, and they send out debit/credit memos to operating companies."

Another special librarian: "We charge back to departments only actual costs incurred—for online searches, for instance, I receive a center requisition/purchase order which I fill out and send over to the business office—money goes from one account to another." And from a food research company: "All professionals in my department charge for time spent on any project. Most users are in the marketing group. There are no goals—our aim is to cover expenses, and it's all handled by internal accountants based on time logs."

However, some charge-back mechanisms seem clumsy and slow-moving. The following tale is told by a retired university fee-based service librarian who obviously did not have the advantages of computers:

Interdepartmental billing was done for university departments, and we kept a ledger to record departmental charges. At the end of each month, charges were recorded; at the end of each semester, interdepartmental billing was done. This meant that only three times a year—fall, spring, and summer semesters—were lists of charges sent to the departments and to the university billing office so that transfers could be made from departments' or grants' accounts to our account. Even though *we* kept track, departments didn't like to be taken by surprise when their bills came due at end of term.

In some institutions, charge backs are handled by the quarter of the fiscal year: "Our library 'bills' program managers at the senior executive level quarterly—the money goes directly from their program budgets into our library budget."

Most charge backs are tallied at least once a month. At a medical complex library, "charges to university clients are cumulated on a monthly basis and billed back through departmental vouchers. The rates, incidentally, for searching are the same as for nonuniversity clients—'basic' services to university clients are subsidized by the library." Once-a-month reporting triggers some libraries to send more frequent alerting messages: "Tallying and accounting are done monthly in this company, but each 'for fee' transaction from our unit [a special library] is accompanied by an informational 'bill'—saves on surprises!"

At an electronics research firm, there is a division—separate from the library—which devotes all its time to "customers" from within the firm. When staffers of this division, all librarians, are asked to do a customized research job, the deliverable is more than printouts and article copies liberally laced with yellow highlighter. It is a coherent, written summary and digest of whatever information has been gathered. The librarians carry out searches, absorb information, analyze it, come to a conclusion, and write a report. All expenses, salaries plus overheads, are figured into their hourly chargeback rates.

At another electronics firm there is a cadre of library-trained indexers—again, separate from the library. These indexers have developed a company-wide vocabulary which is used to index inhouse documents: manuals which instruct customers how to use the firm's products, databases which tell sales personnel which products are appropriate for which applications, and so forth. These librarians' time is billed back to the appropriate departments, divisions, projects. (Rumor has it that the indexers are only allowed to bill back 75 percent of their time: if they work longer than that—doing indexing—they would go mad!)

A few special librarians in fast-growing companies are concentrating so hard on keeping up with growth that charging back seems counterproductive. "By the time something is charged back, the department you charged to has changed its name or the person you charged to is onto another project or overseas or something—it's too much trouble right now. For us, charging back is limited to office copies of books and office copies of journals. For the rest, they'll just have to take my expenses on trust the way they do everything else around here, and so far that's worked. They know I'm one of them, on their side. We'll settle down, eventually, there'll be a shakeout, and we'll keep better track when that time comes. Right now, I'm just trying to keep up."

A librarian in another fast-growth company says, "Sure, if someone asks specially that I get something for them, I'll charge it to them—but usually it's *me* who orders new things and then brings them to their attention. *I'm* the one who puts new wrinkles in searches and puts results on their desks. They love it, and I guess that's why I still have my job. Someday this company will grow up, but that day's not yet!"

At a software company the librarian explains: "We don't charge back anything currently, except occasionally searches over $200. We will probably charge back for at least some of our services, some day, but right now the library's too new—we want to encourage full use of our facilities. Once people are hooked, then we can start charging."

Some corporate librarians wish that there were a system of charge backs in place. Says one, "We should be involved in a fee-charging system, but we're not. We are funded solely by one department, but we're used by virtually every department in the executive offices plus by many of the divisions—someday they're going to wake up to this, so we're keeping very good track of ourselves in case we're asked."

Yet other librarians admit that charge backs are not easy. Says one, "It's challenging overcoming reluctance to pay for information. After all, libraries are free, aren't they? If we go to a per service charge, pricing will be an issue. Too low, and you can't recover; too high, and you lose clients. Difficult when overheads, etc., must be recovered."

One candid librarian, who recently shifted to a charge back scheme, admits: "Hardest is changing my and my staff's attitude. We must not do something unless someone, somehow will pay for it. An example: my people browse 100 or so journal titles each, and route copies of articles of interest to individuals in our company. This uses time and therefore money. Unless someone is willing to pay for that service, it must stop or be curtailed. This has been very difficult for us as we see ourselves as active, involved members of the research 'team.' "

At least one concerned, unhappy librarian is having communications problems: "I wrote a memo to my boss explaining about the importance of goal setting to determine fees. I outlined some of the possibilities, like becoming a cost center, and setting some goals based on specific line items in the budget. My boss then forwarded this to his boss, and the reply was, 'At this point in time our goal is to cover cost and reduce overhead.' Well, everyone who is in business and wants to stay that way is trying to do that. This 'no answer' answer is typical of management's attitude toward the library. If you asked them about a particular *product* line, they could tell you what the goals were right down to the penny."

Policies about matters such as charging back for library services, can—and do—change overnight, leaving bewildered people in their wake. One beleaguered publishing company library which had always functioned as overhead was asked to start charging back immediately in mid-August, and would they please make that retroactive to July first? (You can guess when that company's new treasurer came aboard!)

CHARGING OUT

Charging out, also called "billing out," is a variation of the charge back, and is used primarily in special libraries. Charging out happens when a fee for library/information service is added to the fee being charged to a customer for the primary service of the parent institution—engineering design services, legal services, accounting services, etc. The library does not function as a fee-based service, and yet its fees for information service are passed on to the firm's clients.

Charging out is occurring with greater frequency in virtually all kinds of special libraries—law firms, advertising agencies, research and development labs, medical centers, planning agencies, and more. These special librarians are expected to be billable, to be chargeable, for at least a portion of their time.

Says a librarian in a ten-librarian industrial library, "We know exactly how much of our time is supposed to be chargeable to customers—we'd never get new staff if we couldn't show that we could charge the new people back from day one." Another engineering firm "bills us out at three times the librarian's salary—the billing rates are set by the Board of Directors. We keep time sheets, and turn them in weekly." A librarian at a large accounting firm says that "the accountants here have billable hour goals, but we librarians don't. Our rule of thumb is that we should be billable to clients at least a third of our time, and usually we are. Very detailed accounting is kept of hours and expenses by client code."

At an advertising agency, "librarians are about 50 percent billable to customers. A significant amount of the other 50 percent is supporting the search for new business (in advertising jargon, 'pitches'). Material that makes a library a library goes into overhead."

At a large law firm library the head librarian was concerned that a large percentage of his staff's time was spent on maintenance, not on service to the firm's attorneys or to the firm's clients. The library was totally an overhead function, and the firm's budget committee would not, understandably, increase the size of the library staff. In an effort to "turn this around, we began to bill a little bit here, a little bit there, to customers of the firm. We began charging other law libraries if they borrowed a book from our library—after all, they could bill that expense to *their* customers."

The librarian continues: "Starting to be billable took a lot of energy. There were projects that were done when we really didn't have time to do them . . . but we did them anyway. Eventually our billing was up to where we could pay the salary of one more librarian, someone who would be fully billable. One thing led to another, and now we have 14 billable librarians.

Now when I go to a budget meeting and ask for two more librarians, they say 'why not five?' So now we are staffing to demand. But you don't get there overnight.

"An advantage of this system is that you begin to get *really* good work from your research people. Overworked librarians who do 15 minutes here and a half hour there don't work especially well, don't communicate as well, and don't feel awfully good about themselves. But when a librarian has worked 75 hours on a project, that librarian is working fully to his or her potential. I know that what we're bringing in is a drop in the bucket considering the firm as a whole, but we are carrying our weight."[13]

References

1. For a summary of the rather stormy development of fee-based services in academic libraries, see the article by Margaret L. Breen, "Charging for online search services in academic libraries," *College and Research Libraries News*, July 1987, pp. 400-402. "For all the emotional outcry about discrimination, these arguments carry little weight in the real world where bills must be paid. Online search services simply cannot exist in American academic libraries without some costs being passed on to users."
   Other readings on academic fee-based services include:

   • "University's library fee-service upheld," *American Libraries*, March 1989, p. 188. A for-profit information broker, Newslink Inc., charged Arizona State University Library's fee-based service, FIRST, of unfair competition with private business. Both the Board of Regents and the Private Enterprise Review Board agreed that FIRST's services "were merely an extension of traditional library resources that have always been available to off-campus users."
   • Mary Grant, "Fee-based business research in an academic library," *The Reference Librarian*, 1988, pp. 239-255. Describes Center for Business Research at the C.W. Post campus of Long Island University.
   • *Fee-Based Services: Issues and Answers*, proceedings of the May 1987 Second Conference on Fee-Based Research in Col-

lege and University Libraries Conference at Ann Arbor, Michigan. Available from Michigan Information Transfer Source, Harlan Hatcher Graduate Library, University of Michigan, Ann Arbor, MI 48109. Also suggested is *Fee-based Research in College & University Libraries*, proceedings of the June 1982 conference at the C.W. Post Center of Long Island University, available from Center for Business Research, B. Davis Schwartz Memorial Library, C.W. Post Center, Long Island University, Greenvale, NY 11548.

- Inga Brynildson, "ISD: Information sleuths on campus," *The Wisconsin Alumnus*, March/April 1987, pp. 4-5. An interview with Fran Wood, founder and director of the Information Services Division at the University of Wisconsin. Describes an online search carried out during the interview for the article, and gives details about other "typical" jobs. Discussion of how computers have streamlined ISD information services over its 20-year history.

- "Checklist prepared to assist libraries considering fee-based reference service," *RASD Update*, January/March 1987, v. 8 #1, pp. 3-4. Compiled from suggestions made by the RASD Fee-Based Reference Services Committee and the ACRL manual for the continuing education course on academic library fee-based services (see details below—manual is by Barbara Stump.)

- Arthur Curley, ed., "Fees for library service: current practice & future policy," vol. 8, no. 4 (1986), *Collection Building*, Neal-Schuman Publishers. Presents NCLIS study on role of fees in academic and public libraries (see below). Gives responses from academic librarians, public librarians, and library and information science educators, as well as from publishers, consultants, and association executives. Substantial bibliography.

- National Commission for Libraries and Information Science, *The role of fees in supporting library and information services in public and academic libraries*, April 1985. An overview of charging fees. Discusses mechanisms and rationale for setting prices, arguments for and against fees, types of services for which libraries are charging fees. Presents selected summaries of recent studies on the use of fees in public and academic libraries. NCLIS, GSA Regional Office, Building 5, 7th & D Sts. SW, Washington DC 20034. ERIC, # ED 258 584. See *Collection Building*, above.

- Ian R.M. Mowat and Sheila E. Cannell, "Charges for online searches in university libraries: followup to 1981 survey," *Journal of Librarianship*, July 1986, pp. 193-211. Policy and attitudes of United Kingdom university libraries.
- Ellis Mount, ed., *Fee-Based Services in Sci-Tech Libraries*, The Haworth Press, 1984. The first 30+ pages are devoted to three separate articles on fee-based services: Georgia Institute of Technology; Massachusetts Institute of Technology; and health sciences libraries.
- Barbara Stump, "Operating and marketing fee-based services in academic libraries—a small business approach." ACRL/ ALA, ACRL Publications, 50 East Huron St., Chicago, IL 60611, 1983. Course notes for Association of College and Research Libraries continuing education course 108a, as presented by the former director of the Regional Information & Communication Exchange (RICE) at Rice University, Texas.
- Charles J. Popovich, issue editor, "Fee-based information services in academic and public libraries," *Drexel Library Quarterly*, Fall 1983. A collection of seven major articles on fee-based services, an outgrowth of 1982 C.W. Post conference mentioned above. Case studies of Cleveland Public Library, Minneapolis Public Library, Georgia Institute of Technology, Long Island University.
- Miriam A. Drake, *User Fees: A Practical Perspective*, Libraries Unlimited, 1981, discusses fees in public, academic and special libraries. Chapters include "Fee for service in libraries" by Ms. Drake; "Charging policies for on-line service in the Big Ten universities," by Sandra H. Rouse; "The allocation of resources: an economist's view on libraries," by Richard L. Pfister; "What's a nice lady like you doing behind the cash register?" by Fay M. Blake.
- Accepted for publication in the journal *Infomediary* is a substantial article, "Nuts & bolts guide to fee-based document supply," a "task-by-task guide to the daily work flow in document supply, an itemization of the controlling factors that help shape the policies and procedures that underlie the day-to-day operations, and an illustration of how these factors were applied at . . ." two separate fee-based services at the University of Minnesota. Information from the authors: Donna Rubin, ESTIS, Univ. of Minnesota, 117 Pleasant St. S.E., Minneapolis, Minn. 55455; or Jacqueline Wolff, BIOMED, Univ. of Minneso-

ta, 305 Diehl Hall, 505 Essex St. S.E., Minneapolis, Minn. 55455-0334; or from Susan Klement, editor of *Infomediary*, 48 Inglewood Drive, Toronto, Ontario, Canada M4T 1G9.

2. From a working manuscript of Frances K. Wood's "Dollars and information services," a talk about the Information Services Division at the Kurt F. Wendt Library at the University of Wisconsin in Madison. The final version of the manuscript is published in *Fee-Based Services: Issues and Answers*, cited above.

3. Readings on public library fee-based services include:

   - Barbara Smith, "A strategic approach to online user fees in public libraries," *Library Journal*, 1 February 1989, pp. 33-36. "The issue for public libraries is to appropriate their resources efficiently so as to provide the variety and level of services consistent with the needs of its patrons." The reference librarian is the one who decides if and when an online search is needed in order to answer a reference question: online mechanisms are simply another reference tool provided by the library.
   - Mary Jo Lynch, *Non-Tax Sources of Revenue for Public Libraries*, ALA Publishing Services, 1988. Reflects a 1987 survey of a nation-wide sample of public libraries of all sizes. The larger the population, the more likely its library offered online searching—9 percent of smallest libraries to 68.9 percent of largest. Slightly over half (56.3%) of these libraries charged fees for searching, and most of those (89.6%) offered some free service—such as Maryland public libraries, where the first ten minutes are free.
   - Linda Crismond, "The future of public library services," *Library Journal*, 15 November 1986, pp. 42-49. Speculation is that it "will be very surprising if fees in most libraries account for even ten percent of the total budget by the year 2000."
   - Richard G. Ackeroyd, Jr., "Denver Public Library's nonresident fee policy," *Public Library Quarterly*, Spring 1983, pp. 17-27. About Denver Public Library's restricting nonresidents' use by charging for library cards. While charging fees caused enormous controversy, the action drew state-wide attention to DPL's problems.
   - Herbert White, "Who pays for 'peripheral' services, and what are they anyway?" *American Libraries*, Jan. 1982, pp. 40-41.

"Highly emotional discussions" have centered on ethics of implementing fee-based information services vs. traditional free and equal access to information services and products. Desperately needed are new approaches to budgeting.

4. See J.C. Beard, "Charging for public library services," *IFLA Journal*, 13(1987)4, pp. 361-363.
5. See Ronald A. Dubberly, "Managing NOT to charge fees," *American Libraries*, October 1986, pp. 670-676. Considers alternatives to charging fees and describes the Seattle, Washington, public library's application of these alternatives. This article is followed by "About fees: a sampling of recent commentary," compiled by *American Libraries*.
6. Barbara Smith, *op cit*, p. 34. The ten-ten-ten rule is reported to be used by California State University, Chico.
7. See the article by Guy St. Clair, "Profile: Beth Duston. A one-person librarian becomes an 'intrapreneur,'" in *The One-Person Library: A Newsletter for Librarians and Management*, September 1985, pp. 1-2.
8. Readings on medical libraries and fees include:

   • M. Sandra Wood, ed., *Cost Analysis, Cost Recovery, Marketing and Fee-Based Services: A Guide for the Health Sciences Librarian*, Haworth Press, 1985. Covers cost analysis of and cost recovery for reference services, marketing reference services, "fee-for-service," and a substantial bibliography.
   • Kathleen B. Oliver and Linda S. Blackburn, "Marketing a subscription current awareness service," *National Online Meeting Proceedings 1984*, Learned Information Inc., pp. 273-277. Gives details about how the library at the American College of Cardiology established a monthly current awareness service.
   • Suzetta Burrows and August La Rocco, "Fees for automated reference services in academic and health sciences libraries: no free lunches," *Medical Reference Services Quarterly*, Summer 1983, pp. 1-11. Most medical libraries charge direct costs only, as "total cost is prohibitive." Flat fees are easy to administer. Most libraries have different fee scales for different classes of users. Some libraries charge a "fee by subscription."
   • Peter R. Rousmaniere, Elaine F. Ciarkowski, and Nathanial Guild, "Bridging the library budget gap: an approach to creating fair user charges," *College and Research Library News*,

March 1983, pp. 69-71. Countway Library (Harvard Medical School) designed user charge system with assistance of a financial consulting firm.

9. See the section "When is a profit not for profit?," p. 74.
10. Carolyn G. Weaver, "Free online reference and fee-based online search services: allies, not antagonists," *Reference Quarterly*, Fall/Winter 1982, pp. 111-118.
11. Brochure for F.I.L.L.S. (Fast Inter Library Loans and Statistics) from MacNeal Hospital, 3249 South Oak Park Avenue, Berwyn, IL 60402.
12. The quotation is from notes for a talk, "Creating information services: capitalizing on your collections," given by Lois A. Remeikis on 23 September 1988 at Western Michigan University for the Alberta L. Brown Lecture Series. Details on the database FINIS (Financial Industry Information Service) are available from Information Services Department, Bank Marketing Association, 309 West Washington St., Chicago, IL 60606.
13. See the article by Charles E. Kregel, Jr. and Sally J. Howard, "Charging clients for information specialist time: toward improved library service, overhead reduction and fairness in billing," *Law Office Economics and Management*, Winter 1987, pp. 460-469. Also, see the discussion between Sally J. Howard and Susanne E. Gehringer, "Interlibrary loans: fee or free?," in the Law Librarians' Society of Washington DC's newsletter, *Law Library Lights*, November/December 1986, pp. 17-20.

• Another article about law libraries is Walter E. Doherty's "How to turn a library into a profit center: the law library example" in *The Bottom Line*, Vol. 2, No. 4, pp. 28-29. Emphasizes planning. Among billables: librarians' time; staff time; copying; online and communications charges; messenger services; telephone charges; watch services (i.e., watching the literature for specific subjects). "Don't be afraid to ask attorneys for clients' names and numbers. . . . If the attorneys do *not* give you this information, the costs should be billed back to their business accounts; that provides a remarkable incentive for cooperation."

3
Planning

A written plan for a fee-based service is an absolute necessity. It will be used as a management tool to get the service up and running.

The plan is a roadmap, leading from the here and now to the goal. While writing it, the plan will inevitably shift and change. Even the original goal may change during planning time. In fact, it can become obvious during planning that establishing a fee-based service simply will not work for a variety of reasons: timing, space, personnel, money, philosophical disagreement, lack of market, etc., and the idea is scrapped.

Planning a fee-based service, no matter how modest the service is to be, is much like putting together a plan for a business: a jigsaw of "what ifs" are arranged and rearranged and as one jigsaw piece changes shape, so must that of the piece next to it. All this takes time and patience, and calls for skills sometimes unfamiliar to those doing the planning. As one librarian puts it, "Academics, such as myself, have very limited experience in this area."

The plan is not arrived at either quickly or easily. Combinations of ideas are considered and rejected and recombined. There is always compromise, melding, merging. Many elements must be thought about and worked out virtually simultaneously. By the time a plan appears to be complete, something else always seems to need revision, rethinking, or rescheduling. No plan is perfect and no plan is static or set in cement. As one seasoned fee-based service director from a state university says, "There are many factors you *cannot* control and you must be aware that changing your plan as you go along is necessary if you are to serve clients. You can get new (or old) clients with new needs, or there is new technology or new resources. Things change all the time."

Responsibility for preparing the plan varies among institutions. The job may fall to the library director or assistant director. A member of the library's reference department may do the planning, or a staff member may be hired specifically to plan the service and then remain on the staff to carry out the plan. Help is available in other parts of the institution—treasurer's office, business office, planning office, etc. Often consultants are hired to help with planning.

A popular way of starting to plan for a fee-based service uses time-proven newspaper reporting techniques to formulate questions of who, what, when, where, why and how. Once questions are defined, the plan systematically proceeds to answer the questions, one by one.

Among the basic questions most fee-based services address during the planning stages are:

- What are the goals of the service?
- What services will be sold?
- Who will buy fee-based services?
- How will the service be organized?
- How do we handle the money earned?
- Do we have the money for planning and startup?
- How will fees be set?
- What about scheduling and timing?
- Forecasts?
- How do we handle ethical issues?
- Confidentiality?
- Liability?
- When is a profit not for profit?
- What to do about copyright?

WHAT ARE THE GOALS OF THE SERVICE?

The first step in establishing a fee-based service involves defining the goal of the service, and allying that goal to the goals of the library and the institution the library serves. Goals-defining is easier said than done which is why goals definitions are so often neglected, or else not communicated, from decision-making top levels to librarians actually operating fee-based services. A librarian in a southeastern university writes: "At present there are no formal goals basically because the library administration has not defined what they should be. To run something like this, you *must* have *total* support of library administration. There cannot be a 'let's wait and see what happens' situation!"

Another librarian recalls, "We tried to notify everyone of new charges but there were people who 'fell in the cracks' and felt they should have been exempt, which they once were and now are not. And somehow it was all our fault."

Another complaint: "Decision makers forced the fee-based concept down on me whether it was practical or not—they're making me say we can do what we really can't."

Yet another librarian seems to have blinders on when reporting that the goal, in its entirety, is "to keep a full-time searcher busy."

Goals for a fee-based service in a library are defined in words and numbers: service objectives are put into words and money goals are expressed in numbers. Everyone, from administration to assistant workers in the fee-based service should be aware of what these words and numbers are and be alert to how goals are, or are not, being met.

The goal might be to make library services available to groups other than primary clientele, at no extra cost to the library. An example of this is the university library whose resources are strained just by serving current faculty and students. Such a university might have among its goals to keep active contact with alumni (i.e., court potential donors) and to be a good neighbor (i.e., foster good town-gown relationships). Setting up a fee-based service so that all its costs are met by the fees collected, and actively marketing the service to alumni and neighbors, is a way to meet that goal.

As one veteran fee-based manager in a state university says, "Our goals are to provide a quality and accurate service to business and industry, to help the businesses in our state, to recover all costs, and to provide a way to serve people that the University would otherwise be unable to serve. When you really look at what we're doing here, our main contribution is University outreach—our public relations value is enormous, and growing all the time."

The goal of many libraries, including virtually all public libraries, is to provide all service free of direct charge to its clientele. Such service usually includes free access to outside services for which a fee is levied by an outside vendor on an as-needed basis. These services might include access to pay telephones, copy machines, or online databases. Online database searching cannot yet be done by a patron who puts a coin in a slot on the spot, so librarians collect patrons' fees which are passed on by the library to the vendor. Library service has been free, complying with stated goals.

The goal of some fee-based online searching services, some in public libraries, is to recover not only out-of-pocket communications and vendor charges but other expenses incurred by library-provided online searching service. Included among these expenses are the costs of sending librarians to online searching training courses and the cost of purchasing database-specific reference manuals and vocabulary lists.

There are infinite variations of how free-service-to-all is interpreted. For instance, there are libraries whose reference personnel use online databases as routine tools in answering reference questions. Choice of reference source (hardcopy or online) is up to the reference librarian; whichever source is used, there is no direct charge to the patron—all of which complies with the library's goal of free service to all. However, if the patron asks specifically for an online search beyond the scope of what the reference librarian deems to be "normal," the patron pays.

True to their training, most librarians express goals in terms of service objectives only: "Our goals are a) to provide clients with access to the collection and services of this science library in the manner that is most timely and efficient for them, b) to expand current services to new clients in our current user groups and to new user groups, and c) to develop new services for current and new clients." Some define goals in terms of clients: "Our short-term goal is to have all major (by revenue) companies in the area as clients"; "As the foremost library in our field in the country, we feel an obligation to provide access to our collections and expertise for those outside the university"; and "Main targets are high tech firms in the community—our purpose is to build community ties."

Some librarians give broad, ideal financial goals: "Our goal is to serve citizens of this state without financially impacting the university"; or "Our goal is to bill as much research service to clients as possible"; or "Our goal is to take in enough to strengthen our collections." At least one mid-western fee-based service is quite specific in its first year's financial goals, reporting the aim to earn "$30,000 in the first year, preferably six information contracts at $5,000 each."

In defining goals, be careful about the phrase, "cost recovery." Cost recovery means different things to different people. One service "just charges back cost recovery of Dialog and BRS services" while another presents a more tangled situation: "The goal is to recover costs of searches and those ILLs for which we are charged. The copy charges are to be used to buy books, if possible. There is some disagreement with the finance department over this, but everyone pays, one way or another."

Other services boast "true cost recovery," and have as the goal to take in enough money to defray all costs of the service—personnel, space, equipment, out-of-pockets, etc. Managers of such services must be aware of how many dollars must come in each day, week or month so that all costs—from salaries to lightbulbs—are met. If all costs are not met, there is no "true cost recovery."

Other phrases that carry different meanings for different people are "cost center" and "profit center." A library that is called a "self-sufficient cost center" usually is a library within an institution wherein all library services are "billed" to some other part of the institution. A librarian in a research and development firm says, "We can't even pick up the telephone without a job number or department number to bill to."

A library which is a self-sufficient cost center will have as its goal to "bill" 100 percent of its costs (even though the library never sees the money—the accounting department moves the money around on paper). This goal is in line with at least two possible goals of a parent institution: the first, as one librarian put it, is that "the company wants each unit [including the library and the units *using* the library] to know what true costs of doing business are so prudent decisions can be made about reducing overhead." The second goal is for the parent institution to be able to bill as much of everyone's (including librarians') time as possible to clients.

An example of a true profit center is the for-profit institution's library that generates more income from clients than what it costs to run the library (a situation avoided in nonprofit libraries lest not-for-profit legal status become endangered). A "protected profit center" might be a public library's fee-based service for which the financial goal is to recover the fee-based service's staff salaries and benefits and *not* to recover overhead costs (space, heat, custodial service, etc.). One librarian has been heard to say that "our copy machine was such a good profit center last year that we were able to take the money and send three people to ALA." Another librarian says, "As long as we're careful to bill at least three hours a day each to some client of the firm, then we're enough of a profit center so we know our jobs are safe."

It is clear that "cost recovery," "cost center," "profit center" and allied terms have many shades of meaning. Beware of how you use these terms and be alert when others use them. There is substantial room for misunderstanding.

WHAT SERVICES WILL BE SOLD?

When planning for the fee-based service, decisions should be made about exactly what fee-based services will and will not be offered. It's important to clarify what services will continue to be free. As one planner put it, "If your fee-based service is going to be part of an active, ongoing mix of library services, there must be definition of services for which there will be *no* charge—make that very clear to patrons from the first."

If online searching is offered, what definition of "online searching" pertains—specialized or generalized? Will you concentrate on certain fields such as medicine, chemistry, the hotel industry, foreign affairs? Will you limit your searching to an area of specialization or do you want to be everything to all people and offer access to databases in all fields? How will you handle this? If online searching is already in place at your library as one of the many tools available to the reference department, how will this "free" online service impact the proposed fee-based service, and vice versa?

If you provide document delivery, will you limit such delivery to holdings within your own institution? Will you go to other sources outside your institution (either in person or via subcontract to another fee-based document delivery service) on behalf of your clients, or will you choose to point out to your clients how they can do this document-getting for themselves? Will they be offered a choice? How will document delivery for fee-based customers co-exist with whatever "free" interlibrary loan services are in place at the library?

Will you lend books and other materials (as differentiated from copies of journal-type articles) from your institution's collections to outside clients? Will you track down items your institution does not own, and procure them on behalf of fee-based clients? How will this activity interact with existing interlibrary loan efforts?

What kind of research service will you offer beyond access to databases? Will you answer quick reference questions? Will you offer in-depth research? Are you prepared to conduct research outside the institution on behalf of your clients? If so, how far will you go? To another library on campus? Another town or state? How far is too far?

How will you use communications tools for clients? Will you carry out telephoned, telexed or electronic mail market research programs? And if so, will you participate in such communications without identifying who your client is? How will you handle this? Will you provide "competitor intelligence" for clients?

Is the service you plan to offer going to be a quick-response, do-it-that-day or a within-the-week service? Or will you offer both?

While exploring the mix of services to sell and the feasibility of selling various services, look carefully at what other fee-based information service is available in your area and to your market. Competition is healthy and apparent duplication of effort is common and usually quite comfortable for all concerned. After all, every hamlet has its own public library, each school and college its own information center. However, there are some aspects of fee-based information service which might be influenced by other, possibly competing services. As one weary fee-based planner confessed, "I wish I had known that there were so many document delivery services out there— that fact alone would have deterred me from beginning that part of this service, or would have changed my approach."

Be clear from the beginning exactly what is to be sold for a fee. It is easier to add a service later than it is to subtract one.

WHO WILL BUY FEE-BASED SERVICES?

To whom, exactly, do you plan to sell fee-based service? Usually the reply, "to anyone who will pay for it!" reflects, at best, casual planning. It is in the planning stages that your market must be defined.

In a university library, for instance, what clients are sought? People outside the university? Undergraduates, graduate students, staff, faculty? Alumni? Individuals connected with other libraries in a consortium? All of these?

In a medical clinic, are fee-based services for inhouse staff? For nonaffiliated medical people? For the general public? For nursing students?

There is no one right customer mix. Some services take all comers, others target specific market segments with the most money to spend—psychiatry, engineering, and the automotive industry, for instance. Some information services target government agencies. Others target specific industries—chemical or transportation or advertising. For example, an eastern seaboard fee-based service concentrates on "commercial real estate personnel, lawyers, environmental consultants, testing laboratories, and companies concerned with hazardous waste." A mid-west service targets "lawyers, insurance companies, nursing homes, psychologists, and social workers."

Businesses can be strong markets. Most businesses are used to paying for service and are set up to authorize expenditures and to receive and pay bills. Businesses will become repeat customers if—and only if—the fee-based service functions in fast-response mode. Businesspeople cannot wait until next Tuesday for a search to be performed, and most businesspeople cannot take time for in-person informational interviews. If businesses are a target market, be sure that the fee-based service is functioning and staffed as advertised. If regular staff is on vacation, out sick, or at a professional meeting, there must be substitute staff in place and up to speed.

In general, it is better to look beyond immediate environs for customers. This is known as "deparochializing the market." That geography need not limit the customer base is a phenomenon that most new fee-based services cannot visualize. Most established fee-based services eventually develop substantial out-of-state clientele. Seek such customers from the beginning.

To entice and encourage far-away clients, one fee-based service says, "We involve distant clients in the search process. A client can connect a microcomputer from their office to our workstation and make their end a slave to our end. On a second phone line the client can converse with us about search strategy and results. They may capture results to their own disk, to their own printer, or wait for offline prints from us. About 40 percent of our searches are done this way. We prefer to have the client looking over our shoulder, so to speak, so that they can direct the search into areas of greatest interest and make critical editorial decisions. Client satisfaction level is higher. Precision of search results increases while recall diminishes."[1]

Even though you think you know who your market is, it is prudent to conduct a formal analysis, a marketing survey, to verify if the market you envision for the service does exist and, if so, what kinds of customers make up that market. A librarian at a fee-based service in the southwest advises, "Emphasize the importance of market research *before* starting a service—is there *really* a demand? You may think a demand already exists, but when push comes to shove the 'demand' that exists may not represent an especially large number of customers with real money to spend."

Using surveys for market research is a common method to identify your clientele.[2] Mail can be used to survey a distinct group, such as local businesses, since mailing lists are commonly available for purchase. The mailing should consist of a cover letter explaining the purpose of the inquiry, a questionnaire (get help—they're hard to write), and a stamped, self-addressed reply envelope. Response to mail surveys runs from 1 percent to about 15 percent—the average is 3 percent.

Personal interviews of current and prospective customers is another market research method, although interviewers need training and instruction to be effective. Telephone interviewing probably is the easiest to control and to carry out— again, get help in working out techniques.

One university began its market research with secondary research (checking census data, analyzing existing library-user surveys, looking at levels of library borrowing and lending for categories of patrons, identifying firms and companies in their "trading area," identifying other nearby fee-based services, etc.). Then they performed such primary research as mail and telephone surveys, questionnaires, on-the-spot interviews, etc. The results of all this research indicated that there was, indeed, a sufficient volume (numbers are crucial) of need for—and therefore market for—fee-based information services. The go-ahead decision was an informed decision, a logical decision.[3]

No market survey can "prove" anything or guarantee unconditional success, and yet strong survey results permit decisions to be made from positions of strength. A plan for a fee-based service must define exactly what clients will be sought for the service as well as which clients will receive full service, limited service, or no service.

HOW WILL THE SERVICE BE ORGANIZED?

Financially and structurally, will the service be a separate department, a "cost center" or "profit center" (depending on what definitions of these phrases prevail), or an add-on task for current reference department staff? To whom will fee-based service personnel and activity be responsible, to whom will reports be made? It is important to clarify the fee-based service's position—both chain-of-command and financial. *Make* the fee-base service happen, do not simply let it happen.

If the fee-based service is to be a separate entity, the process of deciding what to name it sparks endless discussion and advice. "Give the service a 'brand name,'" advises a marketing consultant. "If you don't have a unique name for your online search services, create one! Don't use a meaningless acronym. Think of a descriptive and attention-getting name for the service. This will make it easier for people to request services by name—and easier for you to clearly identify what you are promoting."[4]

Easiest to remember and to market are names made up of common, explanatory words. Initials or high-tech expletives generally are hard to sell. Common sense suggests that the best names are self-explanatory: "Joe's Tree Service," "Nannies for Hire," "Coffee to Go" leave no doubt. And your clerical staff will, in the long run, appreciate a short, unhyphenated name without unusual upper- or lower-case letters.

Who will, on opening day, be in charge of the fee-based service? The director, the head of reference, a newly-hired (or "promoted") individual? To whom will this person report, who will review this person's performance? Those familiar with fee-based services say that "five to six years of heavy *administrative* background should be required for a director, and helpers should have had three years' experience." Obviously, being a good reference librarian is not enough.

When hiring staff librarians, be explicit as to what experience you expect. An advertisement placed by a law library reads:

> The firm's research specialists provide sophisticated research support using state of the art technology and extensive book collections. They generate revenue sufficient to provide a profit margin on the cost of all library staff. . . . We often have positions available for individuals with graduate degrees from ALA-accredited library programs, and prefer candidates who have excellent communications skills and are experienced legal/business researchers.

What kind of support staff will there be—an assistant, an aide, an expeditor, a scheduler, a secretary? Especially if the fee-based service offers document delivery and/or book-lending, will there be enough hands and legs to get the job done within whatever the time frame is? From what labor pool will this staff be drawn: general labor market, work-study students, students from a nearby (or inhouse) school of library or information science? Who will hire the new staff and to whom will these people report? What turnover rate is expected, and therefore how often will training have to be done and redone? Will the staff work full-time, or will they simultaneously carry on other tasks in the library?

Staff scheduling is a challenge. At a large service, "volume fluctuates enough that I often need to pull additional students, and at other times I am scrambling for additional projects to help them fill hours." At a one-person service, "You're split between managing and being the 'expert' that the work demands. Then a phone rings and you drop everything for a few hours."

There is an infinite variety of combinations of junior and

senior part-time and full-time staffing options, depending on location, on definition of what services are to be offered, and on anticipated or actual volume of work. The whys and wherefores (and hows) of staffing probably will change more rapidly than any other aspect of the developing fee-based service.

Another organizational issue faced in planning has to do with physical space and the people who use the space. Where will the service be located? How much space is necessary, how much space is available? Will the fee-based service be at the reference desk or housed in a separate, discrete unit? If a separate entity, will the service be behind a screen, in a room of its own, on one floor or in a building of its own? Will there be room for walk-in customers? Where will you sit when you and clients work together? Will the service have its own telephone number?

Fee-based services have been found tucked behind the interlibrary loan department (university library), "on the mezzanine kind of away from everyone" (another university), immediately visible at the head of the stairs (public library), behind a room divider on the top floor near the development office (another public library), in a corner of the science room (ditto), and in solitary splendor in a tower room in the oldest building on campus.

Will the physical equipment necessary for the fee-based service be separate from or duplicate equipment used for the library's regular service to clients—or will existing equipment be used? Answers to these, and other, questions will impact on space planning.

Since fee-based services need to keep a variety of records, the following advice was given: "Be sure your records storage area is reasonably accessible. You probably have to keep things for seven years, and you never know what you're going to have to put your hands on." Typical query: "I would appreciate knowing good recordkeeping systems which do not turn librarians into clock-watchers and bean counters." There is no standardized record-keeping system available. Several services use late-model spreadsheet programs to keep track of cost/profit per search.

HOW DO WE HANDLE THE MONEY EARNED?

Who will send out the bills—the librarian who did the search, the institution's accounting department, the fee-based service's secretary? A veteran fee-based librarian warns, "If detailed invoicing is needed by the client will there be an additional charge? Details take time, and time is money." The manager of a new service says: "Billing is standard as long as you send out something called an invoice and follow up each month with a statement if the invoice is not paid." One service is thinking about "implementing a 'packing slip' system [enclosing a preview of the bill as part of the deliverable], as bills are now done monthly and not sent with the order. Such a system would help clients who are planning to pass on our costs to *their* clients." Several services report that, "We have not solved the problem of billing for numerous individual transactions—enormous time and manpower are wasted."

Who monitors receivables? One librarian says he "sees a conflict between a) speedy, no-hassle service and b) insisting on payment before delivery of search results so we don't have problems collecting later on." Not all clients pay promptly, unfortunately—inevitably some must be chased after and tracking all of this must be someone's stated, regular responsibility. As one librarian puts it, "collecting can be a problem—we recommend deposit accounts or down payment up front." Another librarian reports that "a 45-day lag from invoicing to payment is average." "Collecting is more of a problem with individuals than with corporate clients," says a librarian of a fee-based service; "big corporations pay the slowest," says another.

Several librarians report that they are helped with their collection problems by "the library committee" or the "medical executive committee." Most fee-based services depend on the parent institution to deal with collection agencies, if their use is indicated.

A librarian at a community college library says, "A problem that has arisen on several occasions is assisting clients to understand that they are paying for the *service*, not the *infor-

mation. Several have indicated they would pay 'if you find the right answer.' " Another librarian from a large university fee-based service says that one customer "became quite hostile and refused to pay her bill" when she found that the literature search she had insisted upon did not give her the exact statistics she wanted.

Many fee-based services receive document orders via Dialorder and other electronic mail. "We often don't know these customers and their payment habits, but we serve them anyway. Sometimes these clients don't pay their bills. How hard do you chase a $70 order?" One service which had filled several thousands of dollars worth of orders for a corporate customer was paid a mere 10 percent of what was owed; the client went into Chapter 11 bankruptcy proceedings.

How is money accounted for when receipts are received? To whom do clients send payment, and who gets to keep the money—the fee-based service, the library, the university, the city's general revenues fund?

A public librarian writes, "We currently send out the bills, and we bill by credit card, too. The money goes to the library's accounting department. The project agreement that we get the customer to sign when we begin work has space for breakdown of services and their tracking. Fees are recorded as we go along, and are tallied and reviewed at the end of the project, invoiced, and the accounting department is notified. So billing is tedious and cumbersome, but not difficult."

At a large urban public library, "one librarian in the department is designated as having online search responsiblities. That person prepares bills on invoice forms and in most cases the patron receives the bill with the search results in the mail. If the patron comes in, the search is waiting for him at the reference desk with the bill stapled to the outside of the envelope. Trinet and Dun and Bradstreet searches are charged ahead of time, and we have to be careful the patron knows he has to pay whether we find anything or not. All money goes to the business office and it is the business office that keeps track of bills paid or not paid. The money goes into general city funds." At another public library's fee-based service, "we send out invoices and keep track of our income and receivables. The money goes to *our* account."

The head librarian of a university fee-based service says, "We send out our own bills, and the money goes into our own account from which all salaries and costs are deducted. Both we and the university accounting office keep track. The accounting office charges us back $5,000 per year for accounting—last year, that came out to about $.76 per job." At another university, "all billing and accounting are performed by the fee-based service. In this way we become familiar with the clients' needs but also with their internal accounting structures. We then can suggest ways to make it easier for the client to pay—batch payment on a monthly basis, or a purchase order or a deposit account. All funds derived from our service are returned to the *library's* fund (not the university's general fund)."

At yet another university, the fee-based librarian reports that "we prepare all invoices and send out most of them from our office. Revenue goes into our account which pays for all expenses of our service. Our staff deposit the check, keep books and accounts, prepare profit and loss statements and balance sheets." At a large quasi-public university, "bills are sent out with the information packet and the money goes into the general library budget." Elsewhere, "our accounting office bills companies only. Individuals pay with cash or intra-university transfer." At a Canadian university, "all functions related to this intrapreneurial program are handled by this unit, including all invoicing, bookkeeping, and collection. The funds are currently used to maintain and improve the service." At another university: "Funds are diverted to the ILL fund—in this way we recoup some of our costs and increase spending power for our requesters."

Other ways that fee-based dollars are used include: "the irregular help fund," "various accounts as the director sees fit—ILL, online search, memberships, etc.," "money is presumably deposited into library budget," "money goes to general revenues—sad, but true," "checks are deposited to the library's cost center," "monies go to bio-medical library's income fund to be used by the bio-medical library," "invoices are paid to a special account," "money from literature searches pays for vendor and database service bills as well as training and continuing education, money generated by document delivery buys equipment—furniture, filing cabinets, typewriters and an IBM PC for the reference department."

The librarian at a vocational college reports that "bills are sent out by the business office and the money goes into the account that pays DIALOG and BRS. I keep track, though." At a community college, "statements are issued monthly through our office and funds deposited into our restricted account are used to cover our expenses, purchase new materials and equipment, etc." At another college, "a clerical staff member sends out invoices if funds haven't already been collected at the circulation desk. At present monies are placed into an auxiliary account and are used at the discretion of the director, although this may change in the future." An association librarian says, "bills for book rental are sent out with the book. Reprints are prepaid only."

At a medical library serving multiple institutions, "billing and recordkeeping are handled by the ILL department of the library and by the bookkeeper for the group. Institutions are billed quarterly for basic services: the basic service fee includes salaries, fringe benefits, online time, travel and a small amount of materials." At another medical library, which charges hefty membership fees to nonaffiliated users, "bills are not sent, but paid at registration, which must be done in person at the library. Membership fees go directly to the library and can be used for additional staff, etc. We tally literature searches twice monthly, and collect from individuals or records cost-center numbers."

More than one fee-based service librarian, faced with both charging out to customers plus charging back inhouse, feels that things could be handled better: "If a user comes in person to the library, he/she is expected to pay at time of use. Telephone users are billed by the service unit account department, and this department also takes care of interdepartmental transfers. The money is deposited in an account for us, and we send bills for ILL's and searches to them. Money collected in the library is put into a *different* account, and all of this is an example of an extremely clumsy, awkward accounting system! The six departments at the College of Medicine pay for residents and faculty in their departments. Interdepartmental transfers (IDTs) are used for charge backs. The Dean pays for student charges. Bills are done monthly. Whew!"

At a large university with a long-time fee-based service, "teaching and research departments are charged direct costs. Outsiders are charged total cost. We use the indirect cost rate charged by research contracts. The library administrative office does billing, accounting, etc. Bills are sent monthly to outsiders. Inside accounts are charged directly through journal vouchers. These JV's are prepared monthly and the funds are credited to our budget accounts."

At another university, "The library subsidizes the searches, a small percentage, 10-20 percent. Our department in the library makes the bills. The patrons pay at the library cashier or directly to us and we take it to the cashier for deposit in our department's account. The campus departments pay through CPO's."

When thinking about who does what about a fee-based service's money, and about who gets to "keep" the money, plan to handle things according to what is right for your fee-based service's goals, your library's goals, and for the institution's goals. Remember that you are not alone in making these decisions—consult the business office, the accounting office, the legal department, the treasurer.

You may find yourself managing money even though you were not hired to be a money manager. Consult those who know how and learn from them. Let them help you answer such questions as: How can needs at your library best be served? Are there legal strictures about where the money goes? How does your legal department define "cost recovery?" Who is best equipped to handle money? If your state has a sales tax, how is this handled?

Is there a cash register programmed to post receipts to separate accounts already in use somewhere in your library?

Who uses that cash register now?[5] If your fee-based activity is to be an add-on activity for already-busy reference librarians, and if monies received are to go into a remote general institutional account, how will this impact your reference librarians' morale—how will they benefit?

To make it easy for you and your staff to handle money and other transactions accurately, you'll need forms to help you track the money for each job from the job's arrival, through execution, to final delivery and billing. Among items to consider when designing the forms are: your service's name, address and telephone number on each page of each form (this obvious advice is often ignored); job number; client name, address, telephone, TWX, fax, etc.; client number (if appropriate); client contact name and client billing name; terms (when is payment to be made—on delivery? 15 days? 30 days?); not-to-exceed amount; authorization reference (purchase order number, verbal direction of client, written or faxed communication, etc.); date of request, of service, of billing; method of delivery desired (mail, United Parcel, fax, courier, etc.)

Since your first attempt at designing forms invariably will be unsatisfactory, *resist printing lots of copies*. In fact, before designing your own find out what forms are already available in your institution—it's easier to adopt and adapt than it is to invent.

DO WE HAVE THE MONEY FOR PLANNING AND STARTUP?

To sell lemonade, one must first buy lemons. The idea for a fee-based service may have been a gleam in the eye of the library director or may have arrived as city council fiat. Initial planning may have been incorporated as an add-on job for the director, or assistant director, or head of reference, which means that so far planning has been "free." As opening day draws close, however, money must be budgeted.

A significant proportion of someone's time, perhaps full-time for one or more persons, must be set aside for final planning and preparation—and this must be budgeted for. An assistant or aide should be in place before the service begins—and budgeted for. Larger libraries hire consultants for feasibility studies and for planning and preplanning stages—their fees should appear on planning/startup budgets.

Other items on a startup budget might include capital equipment purchased specifically for the fee-based service: copy machine(s), telefacsimile, office furniture, computer hardware and software and peripherals (including those which allow electronic mail communication), telephone equipment plus answering machine mechanisms.

Unless it is to be housed in the heart of an existing reference department, a fee-based service needs its own collection of reference materials, which should have a place in the startup budget. Tuition will be needed for staff training—and should be budgeted for.

The startup budget also should include money for promotion and publicity—printing, layout, artwork, postage. If the fee-based service is to be advertised by giving promotional talks or by exhibiting, travel expenses must be allowed for.

Office supplies—including business cards for all staff members, imprinted pregummed mailing labels, mailing envelopes and tape, and continuous-form computer paper with the fee-based service's name, address and telephone number (including area code) printed on each sheet—also must be included in the budget. (This last item is virtually always omitted, and yet publicity value of labelling each piece of paper produced by the fee-based service far outweighs cost.)

When startup costs are totalled, prudent managers add 20 to 25 percent for "miscellaneous," since things always cost more than expected and unplanned-for expenses will creep in. (In industry, venture capitalists routinely *double* startup cost estimates in business plans they receive for consideration—apparently we all tend to underestimate what it will take to get a new project going.)

In a candid presentation to a 1979 American Library Association meeting, the former director of a public library computer-assisted reference service said that outside funding was needed not only for startup but also for the first three years of operation. "Prepare for a long development period and seek a source of financial support which will provide funding for at least three years. . . . Allow sufficient planning time to design a good service, one that meets the needs of your community, the research ability of your collection and of your staff . . . and prepare a carefully considered and thorough proposal."

Careful, realistic projections of costs were advised: capital costs (equipment, training), marginal/variable costs (specific to job-related searches), and overhead costs (including equipment rental, outreach and advertising). "There is no standard formula for funding online services, and it is not necessary to think about only one source." Funding sources could include, obviously, fees from users of the service as well as allocations from the library's budget, money from city or state agencies, grants from foundations or corporate giving programs or from federal sources. The director stressed the importance of building ". . . permanence into your structure so that the service will still be there when the initial funding is gone."[6]

Many experienced librarians in the fee-based field strongly advise *not* to start up a subsidized service unless permanent future subsidy is virtually guaranteed. In very few cases has such a service survived subsidy removal. Starting out by providing free or low-cost service and later upping the rates when "they [i.e., customers] can't live without us" probably won't work.

All agree that there is no such thing as a no-cost fee-based service startup. Plan accordingly.

HOW WILL FEES BE SET?

How fees are set for a fee-based service depends on the goals of the service and of its institution. Individuals new to decision making in the fee-based information service world are at first excessively interested in finding out what other fee-based services charge, hoping to receive guidance. However, what other fee-based services charge should be only peripheral to figuring what you should charge. Convenient though it would be, there is rarely such a thing as a "going rate."[7]

All librarians agree that determining fees at startup is not easy. Typical query: "Is it better to start cheap and raise prices, or start profitably?" Opinion: "Be bold in setting fees—I always felt our fees were too low (typical of librarians?)." Advice: "Pricing is somewhat difficult, as one must determine a fair and reasonable price, yet recover all costs, and hopefully make some profit. Some experimentation may be necessary at first."

More advice: "Our rates were set arbitrarily at first, which I guess is understandable, but we've not yet changed!" Another says, "Rates were set by reviewing the cost of each service and assessing (as best we could) what the market would bear. This is reviewed annually, but we wonder if that is often enough— probably not."

Says another: "In setting prices, be sure to remember to allow for those time depleters which can't be billed—inquiry calls for estimates, followup calls after projects, training, current awareness, meetings." A warning: "Pricing of document delivery is most challenging because we must accept unverified references—we often cannot recover costs when much time must be spent."

There exists no recognizable common thread on who now sets fees or how. "The Committee sets rates based on if we're breaking even." "The Coordinator, together with the head of access services and the division head, are responsible for setting fees, and prices are subject to approval by the library's administrative office." "We set the rates but they have to be approved by the university's cost reimbursement office." Other fee-based service rates are set by the staff, by board members, by "management," by "each department," or by an advisory board of clients.

Fees are also set by the head of the photocopy department, by the agency head, manager of information service, library head, library director, library committee, or by the "administration" (however interpreted). Still others are set "with concurrence of academic vice president," "by me from personal experience and courses," "by the treasurer's office," and (inter-estingly) "not by the accounting people!"

Many feel ambivalent about fees, and with good reason. "We base fees on what we need budget-wise and what the market will bear. This works well for literature searches, but not document delivery, which is too labor-intensive," reports a librarian at a state university fee-based service. One service says, "We discovered that our corporate clients were more willing to pay higher prices for a product (document delivery) than for a service (literature searching)."

Most agree that while rates can be set to recover direct costs, it is hard to manage labor costs. Customers pay for document delivery, in most cases, via the package (i.e., per document) price, and yet labor is paid for by the hour, and this can be a real problem. "It's essential to set up a fancy network of runners in strategic places on campus so lots of time is saved," offers a battered veteran, "but the problem is they keep gradu-ating and you have to train new ones."

According to librarians who must work with them, many fee structures now in place are too convoluted. From a commu-nity college: "We all need to learn through our own experiences, but the most important aspect of fee scheduling I have learned is to keep the fee structure *simple!*" Another librarian confess-es, "We charge actual cost plus $6.00 overhead, the university charges 15 percent, the money comes back to the service. My office and accounting keep track, and, believe me, our pricing is too complicated!" Others have a hard time determining "when the clock should start ticking—when does the reference ques-tion become a candidate for charging fees?" Another asks, "Do you charge for time spent on a wild goose chase when you 'should' have known better?"

Rate structures among fee-based services vary wildly. "I wish I had a rule of thumb for setting prices" moans a fee-based service director with a decade's experience. An educational research center charges "cost plus 35 percent for searches." From a university librarian: "Rates are to cover expenses and be competitive without undercutting the private sector; if any money is made beyond expenses it goes to the library to support library goals." A public librarian says, "all variables must be considered then it's see what the market stands. We charge one hour minimum and pro rate down to half an hour." A retired academic medical center librarian remembers that "pricing was difficult because we were attempting to recover *all* costs of providing the service—which costs and what percentages to include were, of course, always hotly debated."

Current document delivery rates charged by many fee-based services, as well as by some entrepreneurs, are available both online and in print. Prices at one given moment varied from $4.50 per document to $25 + per document, with infinite variations of copying charges, copyright fees, outside procurement costs, etc., added on.[8]

Prices for lending library books to nonaffiliates via a library's fee-based service vary from a low of $5 to a high of $20 and up. One university arranged "a 'bulk' kind of service with local industry. For instance, we have an agreement with a large local firm [under] which for a large sum of money [not specified], all employees can borrow items from our library. This agreement is renewed annually."[9]

For an example of how fees are determined, the following is a mini case history of a library within a large private urban university. In the mid-1980s, the library was functioning efficiently and at full capacity, serving current students and faculty. The university's goals included keeping in close touch with alumni and maintaining healthy, constructive, helpful relationships with nonuniversity-affiliated neighbors. For years, the library had responded to requests for service from alumni and neighbors. As time went on, however, the question of how much service to give to these nonaffiliated people had not been clarified or even addressed.

Having read about and heard about fee-based services in other university libraries, the head librarian began exploring how such a service might allow her university to provide library service to alumni and neighbors without watering down service to faculty and current students. In planning (which took the better part of a year), it became obvious that the fee-based service should function as a separate unit within the library, and that revenues brought in by the service would have to recover absolutely every cost—salaries, benefits, equipment, marketing, training, overhead (at their university, an add-on of 54% of all other costs) incurred in the process.

The librarian determined that the service would have to *clear* $108,000 per year, or $9,000 per month, not including such reimbursables as money collected from the client to be paid directly to database vendors or the Copyright Clearance Center or the telephone company on behalf of the client—the $9,000 represented money paid by the client only for the *services* performed by fee-based service staff.

The fee-based service plan included offering three basic services: providing copies of journal articles and other documents, lending books from the library's collections, and performing research. How much each of these three activities would contribute to each month's $9,000 goal was, of course, unknown. To set fees for these services, however, the librarian had to hazard a best guess, which was that 30 percent of activity would involve document retrieval, 30 percent would involve lending books, and 40 percent would involve performing research. In dollar amounts, then, this fee-based service's plan was to clear $2,700 per month from document retrieval, $2,700 per month from lending books, and $3,600 from performing research.

Library planners knew that setting prices for document retrieval would be tricky. Prices charged would be per document, yet the people retrieving the documents would be paid by the hour. How to reconcile these two elements and still achieve total cost recovery? Until a certain amount of document retrieval activity had been experienced, the best-guess method of price setting had to suffice. These were the given figures—there are about 20 billing days to the month and the monthly income goal was $2,700. Document retrieval work would be done by an aide and students and their responsiblities included bringing in $2,700 a month. At the rate of 14 documents retrieved each day (20 days per month), 270 documents would be retrieved each month; to reap $2,700 meant charging $10 per document. Eleven documents a day would trigger a billing rate of $12 per document to reach goal, ten documents a day would call for a $14 charge per document to reach goal.

Parallel reasoning applied to figuring charges for lending books from the library's collection: per-book-lent charges coupled with per-hour-worked labor. How to charge? Again, the goal was $2,700 per month income from lending books, and the work would be done by the aide and the students. The same figures as for document retrieval: 14 books loaned per day, if charged at $10 per book loan, would yield $2,700 per month, the goal. If 11 books per day were loaned, charges could be $12 per book to reach goal. Ten books per day would trigger charges of $14 per book.

Knowing that life is never quite this neat and not knowing exactly how great demand would be or how efficiently the aide and students would be able to manage their complicated running-around, paid-by-the-hour lives, the library director decided: a) to set a three-month time fuse on *all* initial prices, on the theory that whatever she decided to charge would be wrong—too high or too low—and would need adjustment, and b) to settle on initial document procurement and book lending prices in the "average" range of what other fee-based services were charging at the time. Ten dollars per document procured plus a per-page charge for documents over 30 pages long, plus out-of-pocket costs of procuring a document not inhouse seemed to be an acceptable rate. Book lending rates were also set at $10 per book—also on the theory that this was an "average" price.

In setting the hourly billing rate for research, there could be little help from others. Hourly billing rates among other fee-based services varied from no charge to $90 an hour, with many gradations between. There literally was no "going rate" at all, and not even mean, median, or average prices would be useful.

The only rough rule of thumb came from the consulting world: a consultant's hourly billing rate is based on the number of thousand dollars in the consultant's annual salary, multiplied by three. Using this method, a librarian earning $25,000 per year would be billed out at (3 x 25) $75 per hour. If, how, or whether this consultants' rule of thumb could be applied to university fee-based research service was hard to know and impossible to defend.

The librarian's only logical course was to go back to basics: determine the goal for a month of research service (in this case, $3,600), divide by the number of hours that might realistically be billed during a month, and come up with a billing rate.

How many hours a day, on a consistent, predictable average, could be expected to be billable? Of course the answer to this question could only be a best guess with many variables— demand (how successful will selling efforts be and how much time will those efforts take?), seasonality (peaks and dips during the year?), environment (blizzards, electrical failure, heat, storms, hurricanes, mud, floods—they happen!), equipment (downtime?), staff (sick leave, vacations, professional development), etc.

The librarian had some givens: about 20 billing days to the month and the monthly income goal of $3,600. Research work would be done by the librarian plus an aide, in place and on the payroll. If there were three billable research hours a day, that would be 60 hours a month (20 days x 3 hours a day). To clear $3,600 a month in 60 hours, the hourly billing rate would have to be $60. Four billable research hours a day would be 80 hours a month; to clear the needed $3,600 the billing rate would have to be $45. At 2.4 billable hours a day for 20 days a month, there would be 48 billable hours a month, and the rate would become $75.

The librarian felt that the combination of 2.4 billable hours a day at $75 an hour was the most realistic alternative, and discussed the matter with the university treasurer. The treasurer thought $75 slightly high (and therefore possibly hard to sell) in comparison with consulting fees currently asked by university professors. A compromise was set at $70 an hour, also valid for three months.

Setting fees is not to be taken lightly. Any fee-based service, in a profit-making or not-for-profit institution, must balance income needed to meet established goals against what the traffic will bear. If a reasoned compromise cannot be reached in the planning stage, it is probably better not to establish a service at all than to start up and limp along against impossible odds.[10]

WHAT ABOUT SCHEDULING AND TIMING?

The amount of hands-on time as well as elapsed time that must be devoted to planning for a fee-based service is, invariably, longer than one would wish. It ranges from between three months to a year. The unexpected easily consumes time—a crucial person's illness or vacation or maternity leave, reluctance (or inability) of staff to carry out planning functions, surprise opposition to the concept, scheduling problems with executive board or other approval-giving groups, difficulty in attracting appropriate personnel, time required for new personnel (when finally found) to complete previous employment responsiblities, difficulty in finding startup cash, slowness of or labor disputes at or mistakes by the printer, confusion about telephone lines, slow delivery of computers, and more.

In general, librarians make a best-guess planning time estimate, and then double it. Opening day may be timed for the beginning of the fiscal year or start of the academic year, or may be keyed to when new personnel have been in place long enough to get bearings and make last-minute preparations. It usually is useful to create a timeline chart—possibly big enough to be hung on the wall—leading up to the target date. Divide the months to come into work-day weeks. For each week, or block of weeks, activity can be indicated: prepare marketing plan, design brochure, place ads for aide, staff training, consult with legal department, etc.

In any case, to make bookkeeping easy, it is helpful to start a new fee-based service on the first day of a month. If a fee-based service is to offer several different services, consider phasing in those services one at a time.

Hours of operation also have to be determined. Will the service be open whenever the library is open, or just during "normal" business hours, such as 9:00 a.m. to 5:00 p.m. on weekdays? How will holidays (and near-holidays, such as the day after Thanksgiving or New Year's Eve day) be treated? If the fee-based service is a one-person operation, will there be coverage during that person's vacations or sick days? Again for one-person operations, will the telephone be answered while that person is online or otherwise busy? If not, will prospective customers get a busy signal or a recording or simply no answer? Will there be a reasonably predictable pattern, such as answering the telephone in the morning and reserving afternoons for searching or retrieving or selling or other out-of-office tasks?

FORECASTS?

How many customers are planned for each day, week, or month—and which mix of services will they buy? What is the anticipated size of the average job? How quickly are numbers of customers and of dollars expected to grow? If there are ten clients, how many are expected to become repeat customers? Half? None? If 1,000 brochures are sent out, how many recipients are expected to become customers? Ten (i.e., 1%)? Five? Fifty?

Answering these and similar questions is difficult and yet some assumptions must be made before opening day. A seasoned fee-based director remarks, "You can't just shrug your shoulders and say 'blowed if *I* know who the customers will be' or you'll *never* get approval from on high in the first place." Most successful businesses have clients lined up before business startup, and fee-based services can and should do the same. If your idea of your customers' identities is no more specific than "local business" (*what* business—the shoe store? the drug store?), if there have been no inquiries, if absolutely no one else is selling information services in your market place (i.e., a thirst for information service has not already been recognized), you should have a legitimate concern about whether there is a market for a fee-based service. In some areas, at some times, this can indeed be the case, and establishing a fee-based service in such an environment be costly at best or may fail at worst.

The exception, of course, is the fee-based service whose primary goal is *educating* would-be clientele; such a service tends, at least at first, to have only peripheral responsiblity to recover costs. However, even such a pilot should have some best-guess goals for numbers of and categories of actual and potential customers.

HOW DO WE HANDLE ETHICAL ISSUES?

Every fee-based service faces and must deal with its own unique variety of ethical issues. If, for instance, a library is part of a consortium of libraries, how does establishment of the fee-based service affect consortium agreements? If a library is in a Land Grant college, how does fee-based service affect Land Grant ideals? If a fee-based service is in a public library, how does charging fees to the public co-exist with the fact that the public has (theoretically) already paid taxes for library service? (This question will inevitably be asked, so an answer must be ready.) If a university president has, over the years, sweepingly granted to Very Important Personages "library privileges for life" (far from an unusual situation), do these privileges include what the fee-based service plans to sell? Will there be restrictions on who may use the service, such as high school students, aliens (however defined), etc.? [11]

Answering these questions—any one of which could be and often is hotly and lengthily debated—should not be the sole responsibility of librarians. Librarians can and should suggest how these ethical issues might be handled, but final guidelines must come from the top echelons of the institution: president's office, legal department, county commissioner, medical center director, etc. Without such guidelines, says one experienced librarian, "our service will only limp, if not self-destruct." Obviously there are neither single nor simple answers.

CONFIDENTIALITY?

The tradition of confidentiality is a basic library right in the United States. Enforcement of the confidentiality code is essentially a matter of professional conduct of the fee-based service's staff: all personnel, from director to support people to runners and copiers and clerks, must be instructed about confidentiality issues at the time of their indoctrination and training.

Some fee-based services have staff members sign written confidentiality agreements, others detail confidentiality codes on brochures and flyers and other descriptions of the fee-based service. Two sample clauses are: "We make every effort to guarantee the confidentiality of requests made by our clients," and "Information regarding our clients' projects will be safeguarded according to best professional ethical standards."

It follows that a fee-based service should not publish a list of clients, unless express permission has been given by the client. File folders with client names on folder tabs should be kept in closed drawers, not in open bins. If papers connected with jobs in progress are kept on clipboards (a common practice), the top sheet on the clipboard should cover, not reveal, information about the client and the job.

LIABILITY?

What if a "wrong" or incomplete answer is given to a question, what if the fee-based service—presumably through no fault of its own—delivers "dirty data," and the client who asked the question accuses the fee-based service of perpetrating a dire consequence such as causing the client to make a poor business decision, to lose money, or to make a wrong diagnosis, or to "reinvent the wheel"?[12] Liability must be discussed with and handled by legal counsel *before* the problem comes up. When considering liability, look into "errors insurance" or "errors and omissions insurance." Up-to-date information on insurance carriers, competitive programs, on "claims-made liability insurance," and experiences of libraries (not simply fee-based services in libraries) carrying such insurance is available from the American Library Association.[13]

Some fee-based services are advised to add a "hold-harmless clause" to their contracts as well as to brochures and cover pages attached to clients' deliverables. Most hold-harmless statements or clauses stress that only information from public sources is made available to clients and that the fee-based service cannot be held responsible for inaccuracies in the information retrieved from these public sources.

Commonly-used phrases include: "The fee-based service ... disclaims any warranties with respect to a search or to the information a search provides," "liability is limited to the cost of services provided," and the fee-based service "is not responsible for damages either incidental or consequential arising out of reliance on information gathered." A hard-nosed example: "Services are offered on a best-efforts basis. The client may cancel at any time, but will be responsible for ABC's labor and direct expenses to date. ABC may cancel at any time, thus forfeiting rights to payment for any unbilled direct labor to date, but retaining rights to payment for previously-billed labor as well as to reimbursement for direct (out-of-pocket) expenses to date." A compilation of more common examples: "To our best knowledge, information is gathered from reliable sources. However, losses or damages caused by errors or omissions in the information gathered are not guaranteed."

WHEN IS A PROFIT NOT FOR PROFIT?

Legal advice about what constitutes a "profit" also should be sought when a fee-based service is situated in a nonprofit (also referred to, and the same as, a "not-for-profit") institution. Simplistically, a nonprofit organization cannot distribute net earnings, if any, to individuals, such as officers or trustees—or, in its library, to fee-based service director and staff. Net income (i.e., profit) in for-profit organizations goes to its owners and shareholders; net income (i.e., excess of income after recovering costs) in nonprofit organizations must be plowed back into the organization.

Advice from librarians working in fee-based services often includes: "Be very sure that the literature about your service states that the purpose is cost recovery only—never do *anything* to jeopardize a not-for-profit status." Other librarians report that legal departments in their institutions have a hard time advising about fee-based library services because there is little precedent to be found in legal literature. At one medical center, "our lawyers are turned inside out trying to figure out if I'm making a profit—no one seems to be able to tell me how I'm supposed to be figuring cost recovery. Are the few little searches I do now for a fee to contribute to *all* the costs of my library or just the cost of the searching department or just the cost of the search?"

Broadly speaking, nonprofit institutions and organizations are exempt from paying federal taxes to the Internal Revenue Service, and (in most cases), from paying state taxes to the state in which the nonprofit institution is located.[14] A fee-based information service in a library in a nonprofit institution is an example of an enterprise (enterprise is defined as an income-producing activity allied to, yet beyond the normal mission of an institution) in the nonprofit sector. Under current law, nonprofit organizations pay federal income tax on income *not* directly related to the purpose or mission of the organization. There is increasing clamor, argument and publicity about enterprise in the nonprofit sector, and libraries are not immune. At the state legislature level, it has been pointed out that: "Some states are becoming increasingly hostile to not-for-profit organizations of any kind competing with private business."[15]

A leading business magazine sums it up:

Tax-exempt hospitals make money peddling pharmaceuticals and hearing aids, universities sell computers and refrigerators and sponsor trips abroad, and YMCAs offer low-cost workouts. Their for-profit counterparts are fed up with these do-gooders beating them up. . . . The gripe: Nonprofits pay federal income taxes only if

their commercial ventures are totally unrelated to the organization's broad purpose. . . . Congress is butting into the battle. . . .
Small-business advocates have no sympathy. They contend that
the tax law is so ambiguous that any organization can claim its
moneymaking activities are related to its tax-exempt goals.[16]

Issues about taxes and profits came to a head in the 1950s
when a group of wealthy graduates bought a macaroni company and donated it to their university law school. The university
then claimed that, since macaroni profits were going to the
university, a nonprofit organization, the profits were exempt
from corporate income tax. Predictably, at least one competing
pasta company argued that the macaroni company had an
unfair competitive advantage. This triggered congressional
reexamination of the income tax code which was amended to
allow tax exemption for nonprofit enterprise *only* when the
enterprise is a "related" activity.[17]

WHAT TO DO ABOUT COPYRIGHT?

The fee-based service that copies materials (such as
journal articles) for clients must face copyright issues: with
specific exceptions, all of which are open to debate and inter-
pretation, copiers of copyrighted material are supposed to pay
royalties for the privilege.

The majority of fee-based services belong to and use the
services of the Copyright Clearance Center (CCC), a one-stop
collector of royalty fees. Located on Pickering Wharf in Salem,
Massachusetts, the nonprofit Copyright Clearance Center was
established by photocopy-users, authors, and publishers at the
suggestion of Congress, in response to the U.S. Copyright Act of
1976. While CCC does not itself make photocopies, it acts as a
centralized photocopy and permissions system "serving users
in their efforts to comply with the law and [serving] foreign and
domestic copyright owners"[18]

According to a CCC brochure, "CCC instantly conveys
limited rights to photocopy-users to reproduce and distribute

copies on their own in small quantities and at reasonable fees," legally. More than 1,200 publishers (60% U.S., 40% foreign) have registered over 75,000 publications with CCC—scholarly journals, trade journals, business and consumer magazines, newsletters, newspapers, books, proceedings, etc.—so that CCC can collect royalties on their behalf (CCC retains a small service charge to cover expenses). And more than 2,700 libraries, information brokerages, and fee-based services have registered (there is no registration fee) with CCC so that royalty payments can be made and collected expeditiously—usually once a month. The CCC provides its photocopy members with explanations of printed "fee codes" and with a regularly-updated *Publishers' Photo-Copy Fee Catalog* so that a library's fee-based service can determine specific royalty amounts so *its* customers can be invoiced without waiting for the end-of-the-month CCC bill.[19]

The Copyright Law of 1976 specifies certain copying situations that do *not* trigger payment of a royalty fee.[20] Section 107 of the law, "intentionally vague and brief,"[21] defines what "fair use" is—i.e. when royalty-free copying may happen for purposes of teaching, scholarship, research, news reporting, comment and criticism—with four provisos, all four of which must pertain:

1. To qualify as "fair use," the purpose of the use (i.e., the reason for copying) must not be commercial. According to one librarian-attorney, Jim Heller, an expert on copyright laws and how they impact on librarians, "copying for commercial purposes is less likely to be considered 'fair' then is copying for nonprofit educational purposes. When a document deliverer—be it a nonprofit library or a for-profit information broker—copies materials at request of another party, both the purpose of the document deliverer *and* the purpose of the requestor will be examined."[22]

   Presumably the purposes of fee-based service in a nonprofit library are not commercial, as the fee-based service seeks *not* to make a profit but only to recover its own full and true costs in procuring the copy. In addition, requestors' use of any copies must be considered. Copying for commercial clients need not always be looked at as unfair—a commercial client making use of a copy of a journal article for the purpose of aiding one's understanding rather than for pure profit per se would seem "fair use."

2. The purpose of the use considers the nature of the work—is the work factual/informational, or is it creative? "As a general matter, there is greater room to copy factual or informational works than there is to copy creative works. Without having statistics to back up this statement, fee-based document deliverers are more likely to reproduce scientific, factual, or other informational works than creative works."[23] Films, for instance, are often considered "creative works" and when copied may be viewed by many people at once; written "noncreative" material is read by one person at a time.

3. The purpose of the use takes into account the amount of copying. The meaning of the word "amount" is open to, and has been subject to, court ruling—usually the degree of "unfairness" increases with the number of pages copied.

4. The purpose of the use does not damage the marketability of the copyrighted work (i.e., if an item is still in print and available commercially, making multiple, inexpensive, photocopies is not "fair use"). If a client asks a fee-based service in a nonprofit library to procure a lone copy of a copyrighted journal article, that action usually is considered "fair." Making multiple copies—either for a single client or, over time and (perhaps without realizing it), one-at-a-time for multiple clients—borders on being "unfair."

What happens if a copyright owner (author or publisher, for instance) feels the copyright has been violated by a fee-based service which is in the document-copying business? What might happen? According to Jim Heller:

As a general matter, a document deliverer . . . is liable for infringing acts committed by its employees during the scope of employment. This is true even if the employee was instructed not to engage in illegal copying. Of course the person doing the copying would also be liable for infringement, although as a practical matter the plaintiff in a copyright suit would seek damages from the institution as well as from the individual. An aggrieved copyright owner may recover actual damages and profits from the infringing party. Alternatively, the copyright owner may elect to recover statutory damages to be determined by the court. Statutory damages may range from $250 to $10,000 for each work infringed. If the infringement was willful, damages may be up to $50,000. If the infringer was not aware and had no reason to believe that his or her acts were infringing, statutory damages may be reduced to not less than $100. There can be no statutory damages if the infringer believed and had reasonable grounds for believing that the copying was a fair use if the infringer is an employeee or agent of a nonprofit educational institution or library.[24]

Section 108 of the Copyright Law of 1986 applies only to libraries. There are three requirements (somewhat overlapping with those in Section 107, as discussed above) for royalty-free library copying:

1. Copying must be done for noncommercial purposes. It is presumed that any fees levied for article copies *do no more than reimburse costs* (labor and overhead) of doing the copying.
2. The library's collection should be open to the public or be freely available to persons doing research in specialized fields covered by that library.
3. A "notice of copyright" should be stamped onto or otherwise included with material that is copied. Official wording:

Notice: Warning Concerning Copyright Restrictions.[25]

The Copyright law of the United States (Title 17, United States Code) governs the making of photocopies or other reproduction of copyrighted material.

Under certain conditions specified in the law, libraries and archives are authorized to furnish a photocopy or other reproduction. One of these specified conditions is that the photocopy or reproduction is not to be 'used for other purpose other than private study, scholarship or research.' If a user makes a request for, or later uses, a photocopy or reproduction for purposes in excess of 'fair use,' that person may be liable for copyright infringement.

Some fee-based services add the following:

"This institution reserves the right to refuse to accept a copying order if, in its judgment, fulfillment of the order would involve violation of copyright law."

One university fee-based service advises in its brochure:

"Payments to the Copyright Clearance Center, or to specific publishers, must be made when reproduction of articles does not
comply with Copyright Law and . . . Guidelines. . . . Speak with
your company lawyer about this issue, even if you use a service
which says it covers copyright payments for you."

Another university's fee-based service states:

"QRS pays copyright royalties on articles that we photocopy. Those
royalties are included in our fees. Further reproduction of photocopies supplied by QRS may be in violation of copyright. All articles
supplied by QRS are stamped with: "NOTICE: This Material May
Be Protected by Copyright Law (Title 17 U.S. Code)." QRS is
frequently asked about copyright. We refer clients to their firm's
legal counsel."

Yet another university fee-based service states, in connection with its document delivery plan:

"XXX University libraries do not engage in the resale of copyrighted
materials or the transfer of materials to third parties. All photocopying for XXX members is performed in accordance with the
copyright law."

One public library's fee-based service attaches this notice
to copied documents when delivering to clients, theoretically
shifting onus of compliance from themselves to clients: "NO-
TICE—This material may be protected by copyright law (Title
17 U.S. Code)." Yet another document delivery service, this one
an established for-profit company, states:

"XYZ is registered with the Copyright Clearance Center and pays
copyright fees for patrons on request. An additional fee of $2.25 per
article is charged to cover this service and to cover copyright
charges. If this service is *not* requested by a client, XYZ assumes
that the client is making other arrangements to cover any copyright fees for which they might be liable. Note: Most publishers do

not charge copyright for one copy of a journal article for research purposes. However, payment of fees to CCC does *not* authorize production of copies for public distribution, e.g. for advertising or promotion purposes, for creating new collective works, or for resale to the general public, as opposed to providing copies for internal use for specific clients. (The copyright owners should be contacted directly for these and similar purposes.)"

The 1976 Copyright Law is, over the years, rapidly developing a documented history of how the law has been and is being interpreted. The only advice to follow while planning for or managing a fee-based service is specific up-to-date advice from each institution's legal advisors.[26]

References

1. For information about Remote Interactive Search Service (RISS), contact Western Research Application Center, NASA Industrial Application Center, 3716 S. Hope St., #200, Los Angeles, CA 90007-4344.
2. See Carol Galvin's "Using surveys for marketing research" in *MLS*, a newsletter about marketing library services, January 1988, pp. 2-3. For information on availability of *MLS*, see note 13 in Chapter Six.

    Ms. Galvin suggests the following for in-depth views of marketing research: *Marketing Research* by H. Robert Dodge, Sam D. Fullerton, and David R. Rink (Charles E. Merrell Publishing Co., 1982) and *Marketing Research: An Applied Approach* by Thomas Kinnear and James R. Taylor (McGraw-Hill, 1979). To locate marketing research consultants in your area call American Marketing Association (312-648-0536) and Marketing Research Association (312-644-6610).
3. Tracy Casorso and Sharon J. Rogers, "Targeting Your Market," pp. 1-9, *Fee-based Services: Issues & Answers*. Describes the market survey conducted at Gelman Library, George Washington University, Washington, DC, in preparation for the opening of their fee-based service, INQUIRE. in 1986. Sharon Rogers was Gelman Library director, Tracy Casorso headed INQUIRE.
4. Christine Olson, *Marketing Treasures*, May 1988, p. 1. See note 13 in Chapter Six.

5. See "Cash registers at the circ desk . . ." in *American Libraries*, September 1987, p. 646, for hands-on experience with various brands of cash registers.

6. This citation was derived from notes prepared by Linda L. Hill for her talk, "Planning and funding computer-assisted reference services in public libraries," presented at the American Library Association Annual Conference on 25 June 1979 in Dallas, Texas. Ms. Hill is currently associated with Petroleum Abstracts in Tulsa, Oklahoma.

7. For an introduction to the concepts of setting fees, see "Costing and pricing: the difference matters" by M.E.L. Jacob in *Bottom Line* (Neal-Schuman Publishers), vol. 2, no. 2, 1988. "It sounds simple, but in reality it is a complex process involving a high degree of subjective judgment. . . ." Reviews existing studies of how to determine what libraries cost: "Like it or not, librarians do have an obligation to understand the costs of services they supply. And when they do charge for services, librarians need a reasonable rationale for setting the prices of those services. Librarians set prices, not costs. They do have some control over elements of cost including their own efficiency and productivity."

8. See details about "Dialorder suppliers" at Note 9, Chapter One. This listing generally includes prices. The same information is available online from Dialog Information Services, Inc. Another listing of document delivery sources is *Document Retrieval Sources and Service*; details also available in Chapter One notes.

9. Document delivery sources as cited above may also provide information about book-lending services, and prices may be listed with document delivery prices—check these prices, as changes are frequent.

10. Further readings on fee-setting include:

    * Janice Weinland and Charles R. McLure, "Economic considerations for fee based library services: an admininstrative perspective," *Journal of Library Administration*, Spring 1987, pp. 53-68. This article "provides a justification for selected user fees based upon the economic analysis of an indifference curve model."
    * Julie A.C. Virgo, "Costing and pricing information services," *Drexel Library Quarterly*, Summer 1985, pp. 75-98. Know costs before making pricing decisions. Known costs can be used for a

variety of library purposes—setting fee schedules, management decision making, funding support, etc.

- Richard J. Beeler and Antoinette L. Lueck, "Pricing of online
  services for nonprimary clientele," *Journal of Academic
  Librarianship*, May 1984, pp. 69-72. Also available as ERIC
  document # EJ 301 679. Almost 90 percent of polled university
  libraries make online services available to off-campus clientele; of these, 70% charge outsiders more than they do their
  primary patrons. Fixed rate charges ranged from $4.00 per
  search to $30.00. When charging a percent markup of direct
  search costs, the range was from a 5 percent markup to a 100
  percent markup (a mean of 38.6% and a mode of 50%). Hourly
  rates for searchers ranged from $20.00 to $75.00 per hour
  (mean = $30.00 and hour, mode = $20.00.) [Note: Presumably
  this is based on 1983 information.]
- Harry M. Kirbirige, *The Information Dilemma: A Critical
  Analysis of Information Pricing and the Fees Controversy*,
  Greenwood Press, 1983. Price theory depends on the information center's objectives, the methodologies available for setting
  prices, and how these two elements can be implemented in the
  specific situation. Usually librarians can't say how their prices
  were arrived at—"our users so far have not complained." Cost
  concepts, cost-based pricing, demand-based pricing (the higher the demand, the higher the cost), competition-based pricing
  (the "going rate"), and optimum pricing (local adaptations of all
  of the above) are discussed.
- Bert R. Boyce, "A cost accounting model for online computerized literature searching," *Journal of Library Administration*,
  Summer 1983, pp. 43-49. Computerized literature searching is
  not dependent on the library's collection, it is "demand driven,
  and it calls for separate accounting treatment." Suggests analysis
  of: direct variable costs (vendor and communications charges,
  searcher's salary); direct fixed costs (terminal, search documentation, training, telephone); and indirect fixed costs (su-
  pervision-administration, space).

11. For general discussion of ethical issues, information profession-
    als, and information delivery, check the following:

- Joseph J. Mika and Bruce A. Shuman, "Legal issues affecting
  libraries and librarians: employment laws, liability and insur-

ance, contracts and problem patrons—Lesson II: liability insurance, malpractice and copyright," *American Libraries*, February 1988, pp. 108-112.
- Anne P. Mintz, "Information malpractice," presented at the 1987 Special Libraries Association State-of-the-Art Institute and published in *The Information Profession: Facing Future Challenges*, Special Libraries Association, pp. 97-101.
- Robert F. Barnes, "Some thoughts on professional ethics codes," *ASIS Bulletin*, April/May 1986, pp. 19-20.
- Anne P. Mintz, "Information practice and malpractice," *Library Journal*, 15 September 1985, pp. 38-43.
- Kathleen Nichol, "Database proliferation: implications for librarians," *Library Journal*, 15 September 1983, p. 116.

12. Frequently cited, and discussed in both Ms. Mintz' articles mentioned above, is the Vermont case of *Dun & Bradstreet* vs. *Greenmoss Builders*, wherein Dun & Bradstreet was accused of delivering faulty credit information and Greenmoss Builders—via the Supreme Court—won large damages.

13. Information on liability insurance is usually available from American Library Association, 50 E. Huron Ave., Chicago, IL 60611, 800-545-2433. See also Anne P. Mintz, "Information practice and malpractice . . . do we need malpractice insurance?," *Online*, July 1984, pp. 20-26.

14. As of this writing, at least one state, Texas, has ruled that information retrieved from electronic data services will be taxed. This means that a nonprofit institution, such as a university, whose fee-based service does online database searches for customers must, on behalf of the state, *collect* state tax from its customers. Thus the university and its fee-based service, tax-exempt in themselves, become tax collectors.

15. From a 1987 talk called "Policy: Help or Hurdle?" given by Miriam Drake, (*Fee-Based Services: Issues & Answers*, p. 54). She points out a 1981 Arizona bill which forbids colleges and universities from selling goods which are not an integral part of research or instruction. In Louisiana in 1985 there was similar legislation, and in 1987, the Commonwealth of Pennsylvania was struggling with the same issue. Ms. Drake suggests reference to *The Chronicle of Higher Education*, 11 February 1987, p. 22.

16. "What's a nonprofit business, anyway?," *Fortune*, 3 August 1987, pp. 15-16.

17. For more complete discussion of how "related" activity is defined, see James C. Crimmins and Mary Keil, *Enterprise in the Nonprofit Sector*, published by Partners for Livable Places (Washington, DC) and The Rockefeller Brothers Fund (New York), 1983. In their sample study of enterprise in the nonprofit sector (which, by the way, included no libraries with fee-based information services), only 22 percent derived more than 10 percent of their income through enterprise activities. The authors conclude, however, that enterprise *is* making a difference, and it works for those who make it work: the bottom line is the institution's mission, and enterprise is simply another means to that end. Caveats: only one out of 200 or more in the nonprofit sector is "entrepreneurially inclined"; enterprise takes time; odds of losing are greater than odds of winning; the enterprise road must be travelled cautiously.

18. "U.S. publishers to receive overseas copying royalties," *Bulletin of the American Society for Information Science*, December/January 1988, p. 28.

19. Information from Copyright Clearance Center, Inc., 21 Congress St., Salem, MA 01970, 617-744-3350. Publications (all of which may be copied without paying a royalty fee) include a pamphlet (free) "Now you can photocopy and still comply with the copyright law," a *Handbook for Libraries and Other Organizational Users Which Copy from Serials and Separates: Procedures for Using the Programs of the Copyright Clearance Center, Inc.*, which shows how to use CCC and gives sample reporting forms, a CCC newsletter for users and owners called "Photocopy Authorizations Report," and *Publishers Photo-Copy Fee Catalog (PPC)*, a listing of participating titles and authorization fees.

20. Occasionally a journal will make it easy for readers to understand copyright liability. For instance, *Library Personnel News* states: "All materials in this newsletter subject to copyright by the American Library Association may be photocopied for noncommercial purpose of scientific or educational advancement granted by Sections 107 and 108 of the Copyright Revision Act of 1976. . . . For other [uses] . . . address requests to the ALA Office of Rights and Permissions."

21. Joseph J. Mika and Bruce A. Shuman, *op. cit.*, p. 112.

22. Quoted from speaking notes used by James S. Heller at his lecture, "Permissible activities under U.S. Copyright Law," at Ann Arbor, Michigan, in May 1987. A published version of this talk, which offers in-depth end notes referring to appropriate

sections of the U.S. Code and to interpretations thereof is available in the conference proceedings, *Fee-Based Services: Issues & Answers*, pp. 41-51. See also, in these same proceedings, the talk by Miriam Drake, "Policy: help or hurdle?" (pp. 53-59); she says, "the jury is still out on copyright," and gives details about how each database publisher has a different set of rules about users, downloading, etc.

23. Ibid.
24. Ibid.
25. This official wording is cited in the Reference and Notes section of: James S. Heller, "Copyright and fee-based copying service," *College and Research Libraries*, January 1986, note #9, p. 34. The same wording—or reworkings thereof—is found on brochures, flyers, order forms, posters, etc., at fee-based services nationwide.
26. General background advice, as well as answers to many "what-if" and "hands-on" kinds of questions commonly asked by practicing librarians and teachers, are given in Mary Hutchings Reed's *The Copyright Primer for Librarians and Educators*, jointly published by the American Library Association and the National Education Association, 1987. Also, the Information Industry Association (IIA) has a copyright committee and advisory board both of which keep updated on current copyright issues and practices. Write to IIA, 555 New Jersey Ave. NW, Suite #800, Washington, DC 20001.

Information on copyright issues is also available from the Information Office of the Library of Congress, Washington, DC 20540 (202-287-5108) as well as from the Copyright Office, Library of Congress, Washington DC 20559 (202-287-5108).

4

Implementing

THE PROPOSAL: SELLING THE PLAN
TO DECISION MAKERS

When sufficiently close to completion, the plan for the fee-based service is usually refined and somewhat revised so it can be used as a selling tool to spark the institution's enthusiasm and support. It's important that the proposal be free of library jargon and easily understood by nonlibrarian decision makers—the university president or provost, the medical center director, the law firm managing partner, the association executive secretary, the trustee board, and so on. The library director may want to delegate proposal preparation to staff members or to a consultant. But it is the director who holds final responsibility, who must defend the proposal and negotiate with institution leaders.

The ideal proposal is limited to ten double-spaced pages (some argue for 20 pages, others push for three, or even one). Decision makers who will read the proposal should be able to digest main points in *less* than a quarter of an hour, so make it easy for them so to do—if you don't, you've lost them.

When putting together a proposal, consider beginning with the following:

- An executive summary, including anticipated annual income dollar volume and expenses.
- A statement of the goals of the institution.
- A description of the current situation at the library.

- A brief description of the proposed fee-based service, positioning it in relation to institution goals and the current situation.
- A statement of the goals of fee-based service. (One director of a library with fee-based services advises, "Remind people that most fee-based services don't 'make' money for their institutions—most don't even break even! Goals have to be a lot loftier than money.")
- A description of the benefits of the fee-based service.
- A brief description of fee-based services in other, comparable institutions.
- An enumeration (in lay language) of what services will be offered.
- A description of who the customers will be, why they will buy, and how they will hear of the service.
- A description of how the fee-based service will be managed.
- An explanation of such policy issues as copyright, liability, confidentiality, nonprofit status, etc. (The proposal need not give definitive solutions to all policy problems, and many will in any case be beyond the purview of the library director. The proposal should indicate, however, that these issues must be faced.)
- A description of what will happen if a fee-based service is *not* established.
- An offer of further data, details, documentation, etc., on request.

Once the stage is set, continue with an action plan and budget. Don't call this section a "business plan," as that phrase has different meanings for different people. When submitting a proposal, make it very easy for those considering it to understand your plans—don't risk rejection by using multi-purpose, open-to-interpretation vocabulary.

The action plan and budget might include the following elements:

- Steps for planning and startup, complete with detailed budgets for each of these activities and information regarding whether or not needed startup funds are already in hand or will be needed from special allocation, grants, loans, seed money, etc.
- A timetable for when various activities will take place.
- Marketing and selling plans, complete with estimate of anticipated efficacy (e.g., a direct mailing to x-thousand potential customers will uncover y-number of actual new customers within z-number of months, etc.).

- Billing rates for each kind of service to be sold.
- Forecasts of monthly and yearly activity goals, and translation of this activity into forecasts of monthly and yearly budgets.
- A statement of how many months or years will elapse before startup costs are recovered.

To keep the proposal page-length down you can add exhibits, illustrations, explanations, etc., to the end of the proposal. By definition, exhibits should not need to be read in order to understand the proposal—the proposal should be able to stand alone. Exhibits illustrate, back up and amplify what is in the body of the proposal. Exhibits might include:

- Written goals statement(s) of the institution.
- Library mission statement.
- Current library borrowing policies, service policies.
- Description of fee-based service potential market (use numbers, such as numbers of law firms within 50 miles, numbers of associations or legations or research laboratories, number of industries with revenues over x-thousands of dollars, numbers of alumni in various professional groups or of specified minimum income, etc.).
- Results of market surveys (here is a good place to use pie charts, bar charts, etc.).
- Other fee-based services' brochures, disclaimer statements, copyright statements, etc.
- Suggested wording for your own service's brochure, disclaimer statement, copyright statement, etc.
- Details of planning and startup budgets.
- Analysis of how billing rates have been determined, or might be determined, showing how alternate rates might impact on activity and goals, etc.
- Activity forecasts, based on marketing efforts, billing rates, etc.
- Budget forecasts, for balance of current year, for year to come, and further ahead if possible.
- Schedules, timelines (bar charts are easy to comprehend here).

A well-prepared, tight, simple proposal will receive attention, generate professional respect, and help get a fee-based service off to a flying start with strong support from all concerned. Once a proposal has served its initial purpose, it

becomes the backbone of operating procedures for the fledgling
fee-based service.

SELLING THE PLAN TO LIBRARY STAFF

Once the proposal for a fee-based passes muster—even in
a preliminary way—with top decision makers, it's time to
introduce the proposed fee-based service to regular library
staff members. Chances are that most already know what is
going on, even if they have not officially been told. Any miscon-
ceptions and misgivings (there invariably are both) that staff
are harboring have to be faced and handled promptly. Hold as
many meetings as necessary to give a brief description of what
is being planned and allow the opportunity for library staff to
ask questions. Make sure they understand that the fee-based
staff get paid just like everyone else, instead of getting rich on
"all that money" while (of course!) regular staff (chronically
underpaid, naturally) does all (dull, routine, unpublicized)
backup work.

Let the staff know how the fee-based service will affect
their jobs. Will their jobs go on just the same, or be easier or be
harder, or be eliminated (i.e., will they be fired?—most dare
not ask)? If new positions are created to run the upcoming fee-
based service, be sure these new positions are well-defined and
that regular staff have ample opportunity to apply for them.

In the short run as well as the long run, staff enthusiasm
and understanding are crucial. Staff members are, inevitably,
great carriers of the word to the outside. Be sure they have the
facts, be sure they are on your side.

PLANNING FOR AND SHIFTING TO
CHARGEBACKS/CHARGEOUTS

Charging back within the institution is different from
charging fees—and yet there are many similarities. In both
cases, a finite *value* is put on information service. Many, if not

most, fee-based services bring in "new" money from the out-side. In many chargeback situations where the library is re-ferred to as a "self-sufficient cost center," money already extant in the institution is moved around within the institu-tion. "Nobody in this company brings in any 'new' money except the sales force," says a librarian in a computer company. "When we charge back within the company, we never see the money—it just gets shifted from pocket to pocket inside the company. But we have to keep track of what we do so we can tell the accounting people how much time to charge back for our services, and to whom."[1]

The phrase, "charging back," has a variety of meanings and interpretations. As used in the computer company exam-ple above, "charging back" means allocating appropriate por-tions of the library's costs to departments and projects. A common variation of the phenomenon happens when a fee for library/information service is added to the fee that is already being charged to a customer for the primary service of the parent institution. The library, in this case, is not functioning directly as a fee-based service, and yet a fee for library service is "charged back," or, as is sometimes said, "charged out" or "billed out" to customers.

An accounting firm, for instance, typically has clients who primarily seek accounting service. The invoice from the ac-counting firm to such clients, therefore, consists primarily of charges for accounting service, which is what the customer came to buy in the first place. If, however, the firm's account-ants draw on the firm's inhouse library resources and staff in the process of serving the client, it is appropriate that a fee for library/information services also be reflected on the invoice to the client. Whether or not charges for library/information actually appear in print on the invoice varies; often all charges are lumped together as "professional services." However pre-sented, though, library/information service becomes a *compo-nent* of accounting services, and is billed accordingly.

Many librarians have not needed to do significant plan-ning for charging specific out-of-pocket expenses (such as online search charges) back to the individual, the department, the project, the proposal, the grant, etc., that made the request. Librarians report that mechanisms for charging back these expenses are usually in place or can, with guidance from accounting offices, easily be put in place.

Putting together a plan for charging back is similar, in many ways, to putting together a plan for charging fees.[2] The place to begin is with clarification: What is the goal of charging back? Why is the library to become involved in charging back—however the phrase "charging back" is defined? To what purpose? Is the goal be total cost recovery? If so, how is "total cost" defined and from whom are these costs to be recovered? Is the library to charge back out-of-pocket expenses only (as for online search charges), or is the library to charge back and therefore recover *all* library costs? If the latter, how are "all costs" defined—is cost of space and heat and light included? Or is the library to keep track only of time and out-of-pocket costs expended on behalf of a client of the firm, so that the accounting office can figure details and tack a "library services" component onto the client's bill?

Obviously, when a library is part of a larger organization, it is not the librarian alone who defines the library's goals, and it is not the librarian alone who defines what the goal of a chargeback scheme is. Insist on getting clarification and help.

Planning for charging back is challenging when a library decides to shift—or is requested or forced to shift—from being an overhead expense to becoming a self-sufficient cost center. Librarians, especially those in long-time, mature libraries, caught in such situations often simply do not know how to proceed. As one library director put it, "I think we have a long way to go with staff. Many staff members don't like the idea of selling information or their skills. They also seem to put up a mental wall when money issues are discussed. They don't want to be bothered with things as mundane as finance and money. They want to appear 'to do good' rather than have their services valued."

The prudent librarian will have done much of the thinking needed for a chargeback plan well *before* a chargeback plan is put in place: rarely is there no hint that chargebacks are in the wind, and yet changes can and do happen overnight—mergers, moves, acquisitions, growth, cutbacks, new treasurer or financial officer or other top management, etc.

To ease a shift from overhead to chargeback, to deal from a position of strength, at least four broad just-in-case kinds of homework should be considered. First, know your organization, know how the money that keeps your library running fits into your organization. What percentage of the total organization's budget is the library budget? (Many librarians do not know.) How does this percentage compare to library budgets in other organizations similar to yours? How do your colleagues account for their budgets? If your organization carries out contractual work for clients, what percentage of a typical contract can be estimated to represent direct, contract-specific, library/information service? Half of one percent? Ten percent? Should chargebacks be in the future for your library in your organization, how would you recommend that budget elements for library/information service be estimated when future contracts are costed out? Plant seeds for chargeback thinking and planning early.

Secondly, be aware of what your true library budget is. As most know, this is not trivial advice: many libraries' working budgets omit significant cost elements, from personnel to utilities to custodial services. Be aware of the total amount of money the library does, in fact, encumber—someone is counting, even if you are not. Among elements to include:

- Library materials, including deposit accounts, document delivery service, interlibrary loan charges, etc.
- Online services, including training, service charges, institutional membership online organizations.
- Supplies, including office supplies (often not part of a library's formal budget).
- Equipment of all kinds, including maintenance contracts (again, often part of the parent institution's budget rather than that of the library).
- Other expenses such as postage (often absorbed by the parent institution) and public relations.

- Special contracts, one-time costs.
- Personnel-related costs, from awards to benefits to salaries (many working library budgets, including those for government libraries, omit personnel costs).
- Facilities costs, such as rent, utilities, custodial service (frequently omitted from library budgets, and in institutions often expressed in terms of dollars per square foot—how many square feet does your library encumber?).

Be aware of your library's *total* budget, and be prepared to discuss your library in those terms.

Third, be aware of budgets at other departments in your institution. Common advice in the special library field is summed up by the head librarian at a large research and development firm:

> One by one, take the top people of the other service departments out to lunch. Accounting, personnel, word processing, whatever. Find out how their budgets are structured and accounted for, find out to whom they report. You want to know this to see if the library is treated the same way. These lunches are crucial if you are new, as every company is different and you can assume nothing—don't even assume that your supervisor knows all the rules, as often this is not the case. Educate yourself—you never know what or when you'll need to know. Make friends with the treasurer—you never know when you'll need help from that quarter.

Fourth, know what you are doing and for whom. Keep statistics that might be significant to you and to management should your library shift to a chargeback mode:

- Activity statistics might include amount of circulation, number of telephone queries, etc.
- Production statistics could include number of online searches and for whom.
- Collection statistics indicate numbers of documents or journals or books in relation to various departments or projects in the parent organization.
- Stopwatch time statistics might show how long typical library services take.

• Relative statistics might show what library/information service costs per employee, or per department, or per year. How much of your collection supports which departments, what kinds of activities?

Do some counting, look at your numbers and see what the numbers tell you and what the numbers can tell management.

To shift from being an overhead expense to becoming a self-sufficient cost center is not easy. The librarian in such a situation will need assistance from others in the parent organization both in the planning and implementation stages. Before asking for help, be sure answers to the four broad questions listed above are in hand: know your organization's scope and how your library fits into the organization, know your true library budget, know how other departments in your organization are structured, and know your library's statistics and be prepared to present these statistics in management terms.

The experiences of librarians who have shifted to charging back are varied. One librarian at one of the nation's largest companies, says:

> I manage a corporate information center . . . which charges *all* of its costs back to users. All customers are internal. About 25 percent is charged back for individual services such as searches, interlibrary loans, documents, translations, etc. and 75 percent is charged back on a head-count basis as an annual access fee. . . . The goal is to charge back 100 percent of costs to users. The annual "selling" of the budget is the biggest challenge. We have to obtain the agreement of all user groups to pay the anticipated costs for the coming year. We have worked gradually to 100 percent chargeback over a period of five to ten years. It would have been difficult to go from zero chargeback to 100 percent in one step.

The last statement—about gradual changeover—is significant. There are more than a few librarians who are, with little forewarning, grappling with mandated chargebacks. Remember the special librarian (see p. 34) who was told in August, by a newly hired company treasurer, to start charging back for all services within the company and to tally such chargebacks retroactively to July first. The librarian barely knew how to begin. Charging back had never before been done in that company, no company department had a budget for library services (somehow this had not been high on the new treasurer's priority list), so there was—to say the least— strong opposition and utter confusion. Why, wondered the departments, did they now have to "pay" for library services which until now had been "free"? Where in departmental budgets was money to come from? Unfortunately, this company's librarians had never considered the ramifications of existing other than as an overhead support function and had not prepared in any way—not even to the extent of knowing what questions to ask—for other, less comfortable, eventualities.

A university librarian echoes the need for good communication and careful planning: "When you're shifting to a chargeback system, for whatever reason, warn people ahead of time. Don't expect someone else to have warned them, as this usually doesn't happen. People need time to put library service into their own budgets and to build a library budget component into their applications for funding—and these applications sometimes take the better part of a year to come to fruition." Another librarian says: "It's like getting a smoking ban established; our local coffee shop stated way ahead of time that, beginning on January first, they would be providing their patrons with a smoke-free environment—this way there were no surprises and little grumbling."

Revised or new recordkeeping methods need to be installed when the shift is made to charging back. As one industrial information person put it, "We had time/cost information which tended to lump services together (ILL and inhouse document delivery were not well separated, for instance), and this made things difficult—we had to collect new time and expense data."

Some librarians inherit their jobs complete with built-in chargeback procedures. Says one librarian: "I stepped into an already designed and staffed library. If I were starting from scratch, I'd start small (space, staff, and services) and build as inhouse client demand would support. Our library has a mandate to . . . recover all costs, including salaries, benefits, out-of-pocket expenses, rent and utilities, and internal allocations. When I came, I stepped into a 10,000 square foot facility. I redesigned to 7,600 square feet with the sense that I was to use space more efficiently, but maintain the attractiveness of open space. I'm now looking again at floor layouts to knock off another 2,600 square feet which would represent $80,000 less a year less cost for my library to recover."

References

1. For a description of a library that charges back its costs within an organization, see J. Cook, "Financing a library/information service by operating a cost recovery system," *ASLIB Proceedings*, June 1972, pp. 342-49. The article points out that libraries cannot continue to exist by divine right; in industry, the library must expect to be budgeted and costed like any other department. This author's library budget was based on two figures: the total money to be spent on library services during the coming year and the hourly rate for library charges to enable 100 percent recovery to achieve a break-even point. In other words: 1) figure the number of librarians' working hours that can be put towards "earning" the amount of money needed (i.e., the budget); 2) do simple arithmetic; and 3) come up with an hourly rate.
2. In planning for charging back, it may be useful to refer to checklists for writing the proposal.

5
Clients and Customers

Without someone to pay the fees, there can be no fee-based service. Rarely do fee-payers simply appear, money in hand. In most cases, finding fee-payers involves the process of actively selling, of somehow persuading customers to buy.

Selling is an art that can be learned, and yet teaching the art of selling is not high on the list of library schools' curricula. Most librarians are quick to admit that they simply do not know how to sell. Most agree that doing the work for which the fee is paid is the easy part; what is harder is the process of finding, convincing, and contracting with the paying customer. A librarian in her third year of running a university fee-based service says, "After being in the traditional librarian role of having patrons lining up to see me, it is exceedingly difficult to go in search of customers. The personality of the individual working in this unique area is important—one must be persistent, not easily discouraged and able to work on one's own."

A large percentage of librarians are more than capable of learning how to sell if they are given, and give themselves, the chance. The person chosen to manage a fee-based service is usually the top, the hottest reference librarian available (such as the individual quoted above). Although by definition such a person is likely to be more service-oriented than sales-oriented, fortunately this person is probably very bright and quick to learn.

The new fee-based service manager should look for opportunities to take seminars and workshops on how to sell services. Business associations, college continuing education departments, adult education programs, and the United States Small

99

Business Administration (SBA) are likely sources of how-to-sell-services seminars. It is rare, of course, to find such a course geared solely to librarians; 99 percent of other how-to-sell class members will be selling services vastly different from those of an inhouse, fee-based library service manager. Do not be put off by this: selling is selling, and basic techniques apply to virtually any sales situation. The best sales seminars available are those designed by businesspeople for businesspeople. Managers of fee-based library services should take advantage of such seminar opportunities; there are virtually no alternatives within the library world.[1]

CURRENT SITUATION

Strictly speaking, marketing, selling, advertising, and public relations are distinct activities, although many people use these words interchangeably. According to the *Encyclopedia of Advertising*, *marketing* consists of "business activities that direct the flow of goods and services from producer to consumer or user"; *selling* is the "process of assisting or persuading a prospective customer to buy a commodity or service"; *advertising* is "communication of a sales message . . . delivered through a paid medium"; and *public relations* involves activities "directed . . . for the purpose of creating good will, confidence, and . . . understanding."[2]

Popular definitions go as follows: *marketing* is telling customers what you can do and how to find you, *selling* is grabbing them by the jugular vein and getting them to sign on the dotted line for an order, *advertising* is paying for space or air time, and *public relations* is the free gravy that makes you look good. Take your pick.

Most librarians working in fee-based information services find themselves doing the selling and then doing the work once the job is sold. In operations with greater than one-person staffs, the coordinator, director, manager, head of service, etc., does the selling. There is general agreement that, as a librarian from the Southeast puts it, "Each transaction or interaction with our clients has an element of marketing," but in most cases more selling effort is needed.

The new fee-based service manager needs all the help that can be mustered from others in the organization who are already skilled negotiators—the library director, the department head, the managing partner. At least one medical center library's fee-based service is getting hands-on help from the marketing department.

Librarians in trade associations report that while selling is primarily the librarian's responsibility, help does come from sources such as Director of Information and Director of Marketing. Many other librarians have help available to them within their organizations, but putting the library and the potential marketing/selling helpers together has not yet occurred to anyone. Occasionally there is grant money in a publicly funded institution: "A university service, the Small Business Assistance Center, was given $50,000 to market searching capabilities and has had great success. *Money* is needed!"

Selling is not easy. Says one librarian, "Selling is definitely the most difficult area to master. Librarian training does not include these techniques. As coordinator, I do marketing and promotion—not well—when I am not busy filling requests. I had no idea how much time marketing and selling would take." Another says, "Selling is needed, but unfortunately it is left up to the librarian, which is inappropriate."

One veteran allows that "marketing is crucial, but I doubt anyone has figured out how to market fee-based information services very well." Says a veteran fee-based librarian in a state university: "The most challenging issue is marketing. We have stiff competition. We also have the job of convincing faculty that the value-added services are worth the price." The ideal librarian-salesperson is described by the head of a fee-based service in a public library: "The person who should do it is the person who can engage others in [his or her] enthusiasm for information's value, someone self-confident and knowledgeable about the market's information needs."

Marketing is essential, selling must be an ongoing effort, and public relations efforts are equally necessary. The director of a university fee-based service states, "Marketing is needed if the service is to flourish. We have found that the volume of service requested is directly related to the level and amount of marketing done, so be prepared to handle the resulting increase after advertising!" When asked if selling is necessary for survival, the typical reply is "You bet it is!"

Selling also is important in special libraries which charge back to departments, projects, or company clients. A librarian in the pulp and paper industry says, "You *must* sell in this new environment or you end up with no money. Marketing increases your user base, support and ultimately your viability." The head librarian in one of the largest space industry firms says, "You have to keep reminding them that you are there and keep them aware of what you can do for them." Yet another librarian, this one from a conglomerate headquartered in the Southeast, advises: "Marketing library services is vital to survival in the corporate environment. Marketing here is aimed at management to promote awareness of the library and at professional and technical personnel to ensure frequent usage."

The most powerful weapon in getting customers is the customers themselves. "Virtually all our patrons are the result of word-of-mouth advertising," says one librarian. Another agrees: "At first, trying to explain what we were going to do before doing it seemed difficult, really a waste of time. Now that we're actually doing it, word of mouth seems to be working."

A librarian in a Western campus says, "In our university setting, my users become aware of our service by word of mouth." A librarian in the South echos, "Most of our business comes from word of mouth from outside customers or faculty." A Canadian agrees: "Selling is needed constantly, and we do it by word of mouth." A new service at an Eastern university reports, "Within our first year, word of mouth has been our greatest and most influential asset—very positive!" An association librarian confesses, "We have a captive audience—they tell each other about us."

A wide variety of sales techniques is being used. A Midwestern community college fee-based service uses "mailings, articles in the newspaper, brochures—we've been told that adding personnel information in brochures is valuable." A medical information service in a large state university uses "client mailings to announce new services, plus ads in publications."

A Canadian accounting firm library which charges fees to the firm's customers makes regular "formal presentations to the senior executive committee" to remind account executives of the library's services. Librarians in a government fee-based service "sponsor seminars, attend trade shows, and make personal presentations."

A librarian in a Fortune 100 company whose services are charged back to departments says, "I distribute newsletters, try make presentations at key staff meetings, provide orientation to new employees, etc. Client tours usually include the library." From Florida: "Local magazines, such as those published by a Chamber of Commerce, are a good spot, as well as television and promotional sales calls on local firms." Another librarian from south of the Mason Dixon says: "We have used direct mail to companies. One staffer is assigned as liaison to the state Tech Research Institute. We are members of the Chamber of Commerce. I attend a lot of alumni and corporate events and try to have a supply of brochures with me. If we were starting from scratch, I might consider advertising and greater participation in the various conventions taking place down here."

A few fee-based service librarians are candid about not doing any selling at all. Says a librarian at a Land Grant college, "We do not market the service; it was put into place to deal with clientele the library already had and was already providing service at no cost." A New England medical clinic will do MEDLINES searches for the general public for a flat fee ($40, as of this writing), downloading to their own equipment for printing. "We don't advertise this, but our directors feel we should respond if people specifically ask us for a search." Other nonselling librarians are busy enough without asking for more to do; many are frankly tired. Typical comments: "We tell the faculty and students about online searching but don't actively market the service." "At present staffing level, volume increase is very definitely not desirable." "This service will not be actively promoted to outsiders until present construction is completed due to space shortages and other inconveniences."

HOW TO MAKE SELLING EASY

Virtually all fee-based service managers in libraries dream of utterly effortless sales—the right numbers of customers with appropriate and interesting questions, fast-paying customers who never doubt the value of the service received, customers who come back again and again and send their friends. Such situations may not be rare, but they don't happen by chance: you make them happen.

Since the easiest way to get business is to have repeat business, it makes sense to look for customers with the potential of becoming regulars. A lesson can be learned from the woman who runs a word-processing service who explains that she prefers not to do resumes—those customers go on and find employment and she never sees them again. Instead, she actively looks for "rich psychiatrists writing books—their books are long, and if the book is any good, then they write another one."

Fee-based service repeat customers would include those who need continuing updates on their areas of interest or who are in the kind of business (such as consulting or the law) which requires frequent briefing on new and varied subjects. A librarian in an established fee-based service on the East coast says, "We recommend that a fee-based service soon find a 'backbone' operation, something that can and will be done over and over again that is *profitable* enough in itself to pay the bills. The rest of the work can then be *gravy*."

Advice from the for-profit world agrees: "A good rule-of-thumb for you to remember is the 80-20 rule; 80 percent of your profits come from 20 percent of your customers. If you can identify that 20 percent and gear your strategy to keeping them happy, you will be way out front. . . . The more you zero in on exactly who is buying your product, the more you can pitch to them. They are the easy sales made easier—and enough of your business is hard work."[3]

In virtually any kind of consulting entrepreneurships, the common benchmark and goal is to have 75 percent of business come from repeat customers. Repeat business, then, is the easiest kind of business to get. Almost as effortless to get is business that comes from referrals. Referrals are word-of-mouth customers who hear of the service from someone else. One need not simply sit and wait for referrals—they can and should be sought. Current satisfied customers can be asked for referrals: "We have a goal of getting ten new customers this month, do you have any ideas for us?" is a perfectly acceptable question to ask. Businesspeople, doctors, personal friends—ask any contact who seems even remotely appropriate for ideas of whom to approach.

A referral is an introduction, a foot in the door. It is much easier to approach someone saying that so-and-so "suggested that your firm might find our kind of service helpful upon occasion" than it is to tackle cold a possible client.

FOLLOWING THE RULES

There are a handful of fundamental principles, or maxims, about selling, and these sound a good deal more simplistic than they are.[4]

First, know exactly what the fee-based service is selling. Decide what your services will be (presumably this has been defined in planning stages).

Secondly, know exactly to whom you are selling (this also is presumed to have been clarified in planning stages). Posting brochures on bulletin boards and waiting for customers to walk in is not enough, unless the service's goal is merely to respond to requests rather than to encourage them.

Thirdly, be prepared to explain what you do in words a

nine-year-old would understand. This is not easy; as a group, librarians are not very good at demystifying what they do.

Librarians tolerate and perpetuate hard-to-understand language. Subject headings authorized by the Library of Congress are a classic case in point. Instead of "light bulbs," U.S. librarians use "electric lamps, incandescent." "Horseshoe crab" and "river otter" are "limulus polyphemus" and "lutra canadensis." "Screenplay writing" is "moving-picture authorship" and "social drinking" is "drinking of alcoholic beverages—social aspects."[5]

At an inventors conference in New England there were sessions, chaired by a panel of librarians, on how inventors can gain access to the information they need. One of the librarians, head of the fee-based service at a prestigious local university, was talking with great enthusiasm about the kinds of work he did. He began talking about Derwent and Dialog and databases, added something about downloading after dark, referred to Lockheed (don't they make missiles and space ships?), and went on about research and search results and dollars per minute. An inventor in the audience finally put up his hand and said, "You know, I have absolutely no idea what you are talking about. What does this have to do with me?"

That inventor, as were the other inventors and would-be inventors in the room, was a prime customer candidate for the university's fee-based service, and yet the connection was not made. What would be in it, for *him*? What would he be buying, and why should he pay money for it?

Even students entering the library field have trouble with our jargon. Says one, "Before I entered library school I thought SLA stood for the Symbionese Liberation Army. And to me, 'SDI' only referred to President Reagan's Strategic Defense Initiative—i.e., 'Star Wars'. . . . You can imagine my thoughts when . . . I heard of an SLA meeting on SDI. An explosive combination, no doubt. . . . I had no idea I would soon be learning a new language. 'Dialog,' I thought, had something to do with conversation, not with punching codes into a keyboard. A 'citation,' for all I knew, was a car made by Chevrolet.

'Reference' was something you gave to a potential employer. A 'main entry' was the front door of a house. . . . Can an outsider understand why librarians talk so much about 'Elsie,' that mysterious woman who publishes two big red books full of subject headings?"[6]

Always talk about what your service is and does in simple language. Assume, unless you get clear indication of information sophistication from your customer, that the customer knows nothing about the services you provide. Do not talk down—that is off-putting. Talk clearly, talk simply. Stay away from words with lots of syllables.

Winston Churchill knew about simple language. Those who heard[7] these words knew exactly what he meant, and will never forget:

> We shall not flag. We shall not fail.
> We shall fight in France,
> and on the seas and oceans.
> We shall fight with growing strength
> in the air.
> If invaded, we shall fight on beaches,
> landing grounds, in streets
> and on the hills.
> We shall never surrender.

Another example of clear writing occurred in the 1970's, when United Technologies Inc. sponsored a series of full-page newspaper ads. Many people kept those ads, copies still make the rounds: messages were simple and powerful. Here are excerpts of an ad called "Keep It Simple,"[8] copied from the wall above the desk of a senior vice president of an information company:

Strike three.
Get your hand off my knee.
. . .
Walk.
Don't walk.
Mother's dead.

. . .
If you can't
write your idea on the
back of a calling
card,
you don't have a clear idea.

A fourth fundamental selling principle is to emphasize *benefits* of using fee-based services, rather than *processes* librarians go through. The inventor wanted to know how he and his invention might benefit from using a fee-based service. He wanted to be assured no one else had already invented what he had in mind. It would help him to know how many people might have need for his product; he would benefit from knowing what vendors sell materials he needs. He really did not care what was done by the librarian on his behalf as long as his problem was solved.

Customers want to know what's in it for them, for their project, their company. When selling, stress benefits that mean something to a particular customer. The classic example is expressed by "Five Ways to Sell a Glass of Water." When selling to the general public, stress the benefit: "Water is essential to overall good health"—the body needs water to grow and repair itself. Sell to the frequent flyers set with "Water is the world's most popular drink; 4.7 billion people enjoy the taste of water every day." Partying people hear "Water is the perfect drink for any occasion;" the PTA will like "Water helps fight cavities." And, of course, whenever two people get together one of them is on a diet, so stress this benefit: "Water has no calories." Think, when selling water or selling information services, of what specific benefits the customer will pay for.[9]

Customers want to be first with a new idea. They want to look smart and not have egg on their faces. They want to save time. They don't want to reinvent the wheel. They want to be sure of their facts before they make the speech, introduce the celebrity, write the report. Customers want to save money, to make more money. They want to check out what others are doing, and find out what others think about what they are doing. They want to get their hands on specific items or ideas, fast. And customers want all this done efficiently, usually confidentially, and always without hassle.

Two other fundamental principles apply when the fee-based service's goal is to attract the maximum number of high-paying customers quickly. These two principles are: go where the money is and avoid crusading.

"Go where the money is" (a bank robber's motto) means to seek out customers with ability to pay well and pay quickly. The ideal customer of a fee-based service is one who can bill your charges back to his own customer. A law firm, for instance, bills expenses—including those for information service—to the client for whom the expense is encumbered. Some medical research is billed to specific research funds. Advertising agencies bill search services to their own customers.

A crusade involves convincing people that your way is the right way. Crusaders go to enormous lengths to convert people. When it comes to selling information services, going on a crusade for customers by educating and convincing the uninformed is hard work and very expensive. Although it can be enormous fun, crusading is, quite simply, inefficient.

Avoiding crusading means not spending time convincing customers that they need you. The noncrusader concentrates only on those who already know the benefits and value of getting information help—people who do not have to be told what fee-based information services are all about.

Many fee-based information services, however, have mandates both to crusade and to serve clientele for rock-bottom fees. These are important mandates. The goal for many a fee-based service is to provide and encourage minimal-cost access for any and all patrons/clients. Those who do selling for these services are encouraged to—and have specific authorization to—spend time and energy wooing the hardest-to-convince segments of the market. These library salespeople have clear marching orders to go on crusades to convert the unsophisticated, the unconvinced, the un-moneyed.

References

1. Sources of information on workshops and seminars on selling services include:

   • The United States Small Business Administration (SBA), which has regional and field offices in all parts of the United States. SBA's mission is to support small business and it regularly sponsors workshops on how to start a business as well as other how-to workshops on subjects including how to sell. Since SBA's activities are tax-supported, participation in its classes is either low-cost or free. SBA also provides free counseling through SCORE (Service Corps of Retired Executives). SCORE advisors can help design marketing and selling plans. To investigate SBA services, one is not required to be a small business owner. Call the SBA answer desk at 800-368-5855.
   • United States Chamber of Commerce, 4940 Nicholson Court, Kensington, MD 20895, 800-638-6582. Many local chambers of commerce sponsor workshops on selling which are open to nonmembers.
   • National Small Business United (SBU), 1155 15th St., NW, Suite 710, Washington, DC 20005, 202-293-8830. SBU is a national coalition of organizations whose mission is to assist small business. Write or call for details about specific regional member organizations. At least one SBU member, the Smaller Business Association of New England (SBANE) regularly sponsors one-day or half-day courses on selling consulting-type services. These courses are open to nonmembers for a fee slightly higher than that paid by members. Information from Director of Education, SBANE, 69 Hickory Dr., Waltham, MA 02154, 617-890-9070.

2. Irvin Graham, *Encyclopedia of Advertising*, 2nd ed., Fairchild Publications, 1969.
3. "Small business competitive analysis," *SBSB Bulletin*, January/February 1988, p. 11. SBSB is the Small Business Service Bureau, Inc., 554 Main St., Box 1441, Worcester, MA 01601-1441.
4. Expansion of ideas on making selling easy and on maxims for selling may be found in:

   • Alice Sizer Warner, *Mind Your Own Business: A Guide for the*

Information Entrepreneur, Neal-Schuman Publishers, 1987, pp. 89-97.

- Alice Sizer Warner, "Selling the service," in *Fee-Based Services: Issues & Answers*, pp. 11-17, cited in note 1, Chapter 2.

5. Sanford Berman, "Not funny any more: library subject headings should not be dated, bizarre, or misleading," *Library Journal*, 1 June 1988, p. 80.

6. Scott Wilson, "An initial reaction to the library world (A.I.R.T.L.W.), *American Libraries*, October 1987, p. 750.

7. These words, slightly different from those in history books, were written down on the evening of 4 June 1940 *exactly* as heard over shortwave radio by Carl P. Rollins, then master printer at Yale University in New Haven, Connecticut. Mr. Rollins immediately hand set what he had heard in type (Roman bold), added Britain's lion, thistle and rose, printed hundreds of copies, and that night posted old-fashioned broadsides all over campus. This author's father took one broadside down, had it framed and brought it home. The words still hang in our family diningroom; the hole in the paper made by Mr. Rollins' nail shows to this day.

8. The ad, one of a series, was written by Richard Kerr for Harry J. Gray, then chairman of United Technologies Inc., Hartford, CT.

9. "5 Ways to Sell a Glass of Water" appeared in the *Boston Globe* in the mid-1980s as a full-page, illustrated advertisement for an advertising agency. The agency was demonstrating its skills in pinpointing benefits to customers.

6

Selling

SELLING FOR FREE: LOW-BUDGET ACTIVITIES

A fee-based service can do much selling that is virtually free: writing news releases and articles, collecting generic publicity, generating and collecting testimonials, being visible, speaking, making media appearances, and much more. The founder and director of an Eastern seaboard university fee-based service advises, "Establish the business first. Then market like crazy the first year—you are big news! And there is a lot of free publicity available to a news item."

News releases, also called press releases, about the fee-based service, its customers, its personnel, and its activities can do much to draw attention. It is almost always up to fee-based service staff to prepare its own news releases, although some get help on this. Says one librarian, "Since the university name is present, the university's public relations office has shouldered a lot of our marketing effort and they're pretty good about getting stuff out about us." The media are free to use a news release or not, either as is or as a springboard for their own story.

To prepare a news release, write a short (200 to 300 words maximum) report of something that has happened, is happening, or will happen at your fee-based service: someone joined the staff, you are in new quarters, you or your service won an award, you have a new wrinkle to your service, you have been awarded a big new contract. Write your own headline (this is easy to forget) and try get the word "new" into the headline or the first sentence of the release. Use active verbs. Be interesting, be readable, be believable. Be sure to explain how someone reading the release can find and/or use your fee-based service.

Date the news release, indicate approximate word length, give a name and telephone number to contact for further information. Use double or triple space with wide margins. If the release is more than one page, write "more" at bottom of page one, and be sure subsequent pages carry name/address/ telephone number; at end of release, type "xxx" or "end."

There are many ways to use a news release. Send copies of the release to newspapers and magazines, company inhouse publications, campus dailies, newsletters. Develop a press release list (on a computer that can produce labels) so sending releases out is not burdensome or time-consuming. Include on your list colleagues and superiors in your institution—president, provost, trustee, director, manager. Press releases can be sent to current customers, future customers; press releases can become handouts for meetings, shows, exhibits. Write as many press releases as circumstances allow—at least one a month. Remember, too, that a press release need not appear in the press to be useful to you.

Writing articles is another way to create an exposure opportunity for your fee-based service. A by-lined article can help establish you and your organization as industry leaders. Articles cannot be blatant advertising; they can, however, contain a subtle, yet powerful, sales message. Before writing an article, do careful research about publications in which your article might be published. Only write articles for publications that customers (as opposed to colleagues) will read: remember that you are writing for exposure to potential clients, not to impress your peers. Check writing style, article layout, use of photographs—each publication has its own unique style, preferred article length, and format. Write or telephone for authors' guidelines—most magazines have them.

Check to be certain another article on your subject has not recently appeared. Then write a letter of inquiry to the editor of the publication that seems best suited for what you can write. Explain the kind of article you would like to write, why the publication's readership would be interested, why you in particular are the best person to write the article, and how quickly you can produce the article once you get a go-ahead signal. Most editors will not commit themselves to publishing material sight unseen; virtually all, however, will respond to intelligent inquiry to say whether or not they will actively consider material—especially if they have been reassured that what they are offered will be of real interest to readers and not merely a blatant sales tool. Your article should be designed to help the editor do the editor's job—serving the readership— easily and well.

Here is an example. In early May 1987 a conference on fee-based services in college and university libraries was scheduled to be held in Ann Arbor, Michigan. Thinking this was "news" in the library world, one of the scheduled speakers contacted *American Libraries* a couple of months ahead of time to inquire if that magazine planned to cover the conference. If not, would they like an article? The reply was "thank you, no," with explanation that the May conference date coincided with their June publishing deadline; however, if a couple of hundred words could be gotten to them before 2:00 p.m. on a certain day, they could use those words as a news item. Accordingly, before noon on deadline day, 200 words were dictated to *AL*'s editorial offices, using a pay phone in the hallway outside the conference meeting room. What was delivered was exactly what the magazine wanted and could use; what was delivered was published verbatim.

Do not write anything until an editor has expressed interest in seeing it. Many librarians slave over articles and then try to "place" them. It's a waste of time. You only should write for a source that has expressed interest. Send along a note saying "Here is the article on xxx that we discussed earlier this month—I look forward to hearing your reactions." Your material may not get published, but it certainly will get read.

Protocols for writing articles are similar to those for preparing press releases: indicate date, where to get further information (including telephone number), and approximate word length. Double or triple space with wide margins. Be sure the article name and your name and address appear on each page of the manuscript. Write clear, simple, jargon-free prose. In most cases avoid footnotes—this is not a term paper. Enclose a *recent* black-and-white photograph of yourself, and prepare a 25- to 30-word description of who you are and what you do (to be printed under your photograph). Clip (don't staple) pages together, and send the article flat. Enclose a stamped, addressed envelope for the article's return should the editor decide not to use the article or require rewriting.

If an article is accepted for publication, inquire if you may distribute preprints to colleagues and customers. Once an article is printed, request reprints for distribution. Aim for at least two to three articles a year so that at any time you have one recently published, one about to be published, and a third in the works.

Another kind of writing that brings free publicity to a fee-based service is a *regular column* in a newsletter, journal, or paper read by your potential, and current, clientele. For instance, a column could be in a newspaper's financial section, a business club's monthly newsletter, etc. Make the column brief, interesting, useful. Inform and entertain. Prepare the column according to editorial specifications, meet your deadlines, always be one or two columns ahead.

An example that might have made good column-reading is this librarian's tale: "We had no success after extensive searching for material about an application of an agricultural product, and we were shocked to find out that the client was *pleased*! Now we ask every customer what they expect or wish the outcome of our research to be—sometimes they hope to get nothing at all!" Another example that could easily have fit a column: "A client needed some data quickly but there was a blizzard and *no* mail service could leave the city. We used the electronic bulletin board to load the information for the client, and he pulled the information off in his snow-bound country home. What's more, he paid!" People who read columns not only want information, they want to be entertained. Give them what they want.

Distributing a *newsletter* is a low-cost method of keeping a fee-based service visible. Each issue of the newsletter should briefly describe what the fee-based is and does, who has used the service, and how to contact the service. Never assume newsletter readers automatically know this information. One quarterly newsletter describes goals and services and tells stories about information requests that have recently been answered—from market data to minicomputer brands to ready-to-assemble furniture—and asks, "Do you have a similar information problem at your organization which you'd like us to research?"

Another fee-based services' newsletter has a column called "QRS Requests" which points out how many requests have come in in recent months and gives examples such as "software developments in India, raster image scanners, executive lists, flow injection analysis." Another column is called "QRS Case 1" and gives details about a typical request, such as "effects of ice loads on bridge construction," and then describes the deliverables— in this case six article copies and 68 abstracts—all faxed to the client within 24 hours.

A variation on the newsletter is the *annual report*—not free, yet not necessarily costly. A recent annual report of a fee-based service in a state university is eight pages long. The report thanks clients, friends and advisors. The year's activity is described in less than 200 words with over a dozen photographs showing the staff at work. Examples of the kinds of questions asked are given: information about manufacturing latex gloves, regional rental values of farmland, etc. What is delivered in reponse to questions is described: a computer-generated list of articles, photocopy of a government publication, a referral to an expert. A pie chart shows the client breakdown by industrial sector (largest sector is manufacturing at 40.9%, smallest is agriculture at 1.8%). Another pie chart shows the breakdown of question subjects (engineering/technology largest at 32.4%, agriculture again the smallest at 5.8%). A state map shows how many clients come from which counties. A few thank-you notes are reproduced. There is a one-sentence biography of each staff member, from program coordinator to secretary.

Collecting and using *generic publicity*—and more is being

published all the time—can help you explain what the fee-based service does. Prospective customers will better understand the benefits of online searching if they read the *Reader's Digest* article by a heart surgeon which tells how online searching helps doctors help patients.[1] An office manager might be persuaded to become a client if attention is drawn to a write-up on database searching in *Administrative Management*,[2] a magazine read by most office managers.

A marketing executive can be introduced to "Which database solves which marketing problem?" in *Sales and Marketing Management*.[3] Ten marketing "problems" are posed—outlook for soaps and creams, printing industry top corporate executives, bank marketing techniques on home equity loans, ad spending on retail footwear, etc., and hints are given about which database will have what "answers." A business client can be steered to "The Subject is: BUSINESS—an update on electronic information sources," for a readable description of the pace of development of business databases. This article confirms that effective business searching is not a do-it-yourself activity, it is a job for experts.[4]

Articles on online searching can add to our arsenal of examples—examples which help sell the benefits of online searching. A story of how database searching pinpoints information is that of the person who "wanted to find a *Chicago Tribune* story on a store owner who booby-trapped his store with an electronic device that killed a thief who was trying to rob the store. The store owner was tried for manslaughter." The librarian-searcher typed the search command "store/15 booby" to tell the computer (in this case, a full-text newspaper index) to look for articles that contained the words "store" and "booby" within 15 words of each other. The answer was found in a minute and a half. The unusual question and the clever response make interesting reading and certainly draw attention to the benefits of online databases.[5]

Another tale that made interesting reading and provided a lively, timely example of how databases can help people do their jobs better is the story of the writer who was ghost-writing part of an instant biography on Geraldine Ferraro, shortly after she made the Democratic presidential ticket. The writer wanted to interview Ms. Ferraro's law school class-mates, but was unable to get through to the law school to get names. So he turned to the *Who's Who* database and asked the computer to select "JD" adjacent to the name of the law school adjacent to "1960." The first hit turned up a nearby attorney. He phoned him, and the attorney said, "Oh sure, I knew Geraldine, she was in my study group. . . .."[6]

Being aware of, collecting, and using generic pubicity can be helpful in spreading the word about what you do. Another ploy is to *collect testimonials*: in other words, start keeping your fan mail. If a bill-paying client pens "thanks a lot, what you sent us made the day" in the margin of the invoice, keep that note. If a request arrives saying, "The last time I made a speech you made me look as if I actually knew what I was talking about, so I'm asking you to do it again," put a copy of that request in your testimonials file. If you don't get any fan mail, generate some. Deliver a short questionnaire with search results. Keep the replies, tabulate the results. Was the search delivered on schedule? Did the searcher demonstrate under-standing of the question? How much time did the search save? Were search results helpful? How could the search have been better?

Testimonials and fan mail can be worked into press releas-es, articles, and brochures. Occasionally it is appropriate to ask a client for permission to use material. Usually, however, remarks can be kept anonymous: "Terrific! Saved us days of work," "Our report couldn't have been written without you," and "Thanks for pointing out new vendor sources" do not violate customer confidentiality. Nor does this statement: "Nine-ty-two of our customers last year rated our service 'highly satisfactory.'"

Being visible[7] is a great asset in publicizing a fee-based service. Do not simply hide in the library and assume that doing good work is enough—get out there and be seen. You must be seen by and known by potential customers, not simply by your professional colleagues.

Where you choose to be seen obviously depends on where

customers are. If you are courting lawyers, go to the meetings
lawyers go to. If you seek manufacturing clients, go to their
trade shows and conferences. "Find out where the watering
holes are," advises an old hand, "and go there yourself, regularly." It is virtually always true that you do not have to belong to
an organization to attend its meetings—you just may have to
pay a bit more for the event than do members. Arrive early,
introduce yourself, carry business cards and brochures. In a
group new and strange to you, do a lot of listening and ask
questions. Find out what people's needs are.

When concentrating on being visible, be sure you build a
strong and positive image.[8] Look and act as if you mean
business; dress comfortably yet appropriately, carry the proper
tools (brief case, pen, business cards, small notebook). Stand
straight, smile, look people in the eye, have something to say
for yourself, don't fidget or appear anxious or apologize for your
presence. Make sure your nametag is easily readable—most
aren't and need to be fixed.

Another low-budget method of making your service known is
to give *speeches*. Make your availability as a speaker known
and become known as a good speaker. If your fee-based service
is in a college or university, suggest that the alumni office use
your speaking services at regional club meetings. Be ready to
speak, even on short notice, to professional and business groups.
Some groups meet every week all year and their program
chairs are constantly looking for good speakers. Your speech
cannot be a downright hard sell. It can, however, include
stories—both serious and funny—about how your customers
use your service. Custom-design each speech. Never talk
down: use simple, clear, conversational language. Never read a
speech. Use examples appropriate to your audience—check
your collection of generic publicity for ideas. Always be prepared to speak for a shorter time than you have been told will
be available to you; short speeches are memorable speeches.

Encourage questions. If the audience has none, anticipate
this and answer some on your own. Examples: "We are often
asked what we would do if two people asked us exactly the
same question on the same day, and we want you to know

that . . .," or "Let me tell you about a hilarious situation we got into the other day . . . ."

Media interviews provide excellent free publicity. If you are known as a sparkling public speaker, if press releases about your service are really interesting and not stodgily academic, if you are visible and seen about town as an interesting, vital character, the media will find you. If not, you can find the media. Communities with cable television may have do-it-yourself media opportunities. Beyond that, familiarize yourself with radio or television programs which you feel would be appropriate vehicles for your story, find out the name (this is important) of the producer, and telephone or write saying how much you enjoy the program and that you have a story you feel is of interest to the audience (i.e., show you are aware of media goals, not just your own).

Before you are interviewed, do what you can to make it easy for the interviewer to conduct a good interview.[9] Ahead of time, produce sample questions, indicate what kind of stories you can tell, show how you can relate to the audience's interests. Be prepared for dollars and cents questions, and don't hedge on the answers. Usually it's better to say, "We're very expensive, but we're worth every cent—a job we do is billed at anywhere from $150 to $1,500," rather than to announce what your hourly rate is. Most reporters have no experience dealing with librarians outside traditional library settings. Here is your opportunity to show what our profession can do.

BROCHURES

Sooner or later, all libraries with fee-based services need a descriptive brochure.[10] But good brochures are very difficult to design and many brochures now in use are not effective. As one librarian puts it: "Most of the brochures I've seen are rather poor, precisely because they seem to speak to other information professionals rather than to prospective clients."

The first few drafts of a brochure should be produced by staff involved in the fee-based service, as they know best what is being sold, to whom, and why. Ideally, final design should be done by a professional. If you have access to desktop publishing equipment,[11] you may be able to produce your brochure in-house. In general, however, it is advisable to seek advice from brochure lay-out artists for whom this is a full-time profession. There are many, many adequate brochures describing fee-based services. There are few that are excellent, and these are produced by people who really know how.

Many fee-based services are located in institutions which ha·,e public relations or marketing departments—ask them for help. Whether you work with an outside designer or deal with the inhouse public relations or marketing people, if you find yourself frustrated that they "don't understand about information service," the fault is most likely yours. If you can't explain what you want to the person who is doing your brochure, chances are that you are not using simple enough language.

A successful brochure will get the attention of real customer prospects because it contains useful, pertinent, and interest-provoking information. When preparing your first draft, consider including the following:

1. Name of service, name of library, name of university.
2. Mailing address of service, including zip code.
3. Physical location of service (room number, floor number), if different from mailing address.
4. Telephone number, including area code, as well as other communications details as applicable (fax, electronic mail, etc.). Indicate if an answering machine or service monitors incoming telephone calls during off hours.
5. Description of clientele who benefit from fee-based service (such as "created for organizations and individuals not affiliated with the university," or "open to all residents of Woodbridge," or "especially designed as a unique service exclusively for association members").
6. Days of the week and hours the service is open. Is the service open whenever the library is open? Holidays? Nights? Weekends? Emergency service?
7. Statement of goals, especially if fee-based service is in a non-

profit institution. Example: "Operates on a cost-recovery, not-for-profit basis."

8. Description of each kind of service offered and the schedule of fees. Include information on how expenses (database and communications charges, copyright fees, shipping charges, etc.) are handled.

9. Details of when and how bills are submitted (delivered with search results, mailed each Monday for work performed the previous week, etc.).

10. Payment terms ("on delivery" or "net 15 days," etc.).

11. How checks should be made out.

12. Description of how services can be charged to in-house departments, projects, etc.

13. Reassurance that, while it is impossible to forecast research costs exactly, the fee-based service can give cost estimates which will not be exceeded without express client permission.

14. Indication of how quickly the fee-based service can normally respond to requests, as well as description of rush service option and its costs (usually 50 percent to 100 percent surcharge of regular charges).

15. Explanation of any two-tiered or multi-tiered fee structures—such as one fee for university affiliates, another for alumni, and a third for nonaffiliates. Another example, in a membership organization, there would be one fee for members and a higher fee for nonmembers.

16. Reassurance that confidentiality of client requests will be honored.

17. Specific date until which stated fees are valid. This is better than a generic "fees can change without notice" statement.

18. Abbreviated "best-efforts statement" or "hold-harmless clause" (if legal counsel so advises).

19. Photographs—of people at work, of a customer receiving an information packet, of the sign over the door, of the building, etc.

The words and phrases you choose to describe your services on the brochure must be simple and clear and understandable. Avoid jargon, and you'll avoid confusion. "Copies of journal articles" is easier to understand than "document retrieval" or "document delivery" (what's a document, anyway?). Differentiate between copying from journals available in the library and copying from journals which must be procured elsewhere. Don't use library jargon, such as Interlibrary Loan or ILL.

When describing your charges for research, indicate how the hourly fee is computed (such as "one-hour minimum, billed thereafter in quarter-hour increments"). Indicate how out-of-pocket expenses (database and communications charges, copyright fees, etc.) will be billed: at cost or at cost plus a percent service charge. Is there a standard shipping charge? Be very, very clear.

When you have finally finished the agonizing process of writing a brochure's first draft, seek reviews from people *outside* the library/information professions. Ideally, show the brochure draft to potential customers, and see what their reaction is. If they don't understand it, you've not written clearly enough. If that is the case, start again. Do not rely solely on your library colleagues' opinions—they will, understandably, be wearing professional blinders and will not be able to judge the brochure through novice eyes. They are used to our jargon, our comfortable language shortcuts and acronyms and will not spot them as danger signals.

An examination of brochures currently in use by fee-based information services shows that many emphasize benefits to customers. An example: "In your own work, you need authoritative and current information to make important decisions, some with far-reaching consequences, as well as for immediate use. Usually the information you need must be in your hands quickly and at reasonable cost. We, at ABC, can meet those needs." Another example:

> The XYZ shortcut—it will save your company time and money, while making your life easier. . . . In many cases, you and your competitors are trying to find the same critical answers. With XYZ, you'll arrive first. . . . By taking the XYZ shortcut, you can identify and locate new materials, find new suppliers, solve product performance or manufacturing problems, lower development and production costs, search existing patents and monitor patent activity, learn about codes and regulations and compliance, determine whether to "make" or "buy," bring new products to the market

faster, become instantly knowledgeable in unfamiliar or emerging technologies. . . . With XYZ, you'll never again have to face a technical problem or difficult technical decision alone.

Here are other brochure examples emphasizing benefits: "QRS' swift retrieval of information will allow you to use your time in the most productive way possible. . . . QRS provides you with fast expert service. Whatever your needs, you can always expect quick delivery. . . ." Another:

> Success in today's business world depends on the right information at the right time. The team of professionals at GEF helps you save time, effort and money by providing the information you need when you need it. GEF locates and delivers information to you within *your* time frame—by mail or by overnight express service. . . . The cost of using GEF's service is less than it would be for you or your employees to determine the source of information and obtain it. This is because our business is information—it's what we deal with every day.

Yet another brochure highlights service benefits: "HIJ is simple to use, HIJ is confidential, HIJ is dedicated to prompt service, HIJ's fees are reasonable, for more information call HIJ at . . ."

Examples of what kinds of service have been and can be performed appear on some brochures. One lists "a brief overview of services we provide." Another stresses activity: "ABC brings the Library to you by providing *access* to a journal collection of x,000 titles, *books* from the Library's collection of xxx,000, *photocopies* of materials in the Library's collection, *loan* of materials from other institutions, *patents and standards* both domestic and foreign, *computerized searching* of international databases," etc.

Other brochures are designed around what a client may ask for and do. For instance: "Attorneys are welcome to use the library. Do not hesitate to ask a member of the library staff for reference assistance. Library staff will photocopy materials for you. . . . Library staff will answer ready-reference questions for you. . . . While we do not have staff to do in-depth research for attorneys, we will refer such questions to law students who want to work on research projects. . . ."

Some brochures list specific questions and problems. "Do you want to know . . . what is a company's liability for a defective product? How cost-effective is word-processing equipment? Who is doing research in your field? Call us."

Another brochure gives a sampling of past requests, including: "Have any articles been published concerning the history of the candy industry?," "What are hotels and motels doing about the security and safety of their guests?," "What was the market share for diet soft drinks in 1985?," and "What is the FDA position regarding tamper-evident closures for food?"

Yet another brochure describing the services of a database vendor, asks readers to take a quiz—"How much professional literature can *you* review in a month? How long would it take you to make a list of bibliographic references to material published since 1965 on the subject of xxx?"—then points out the very few minutes it would take, using their fee-based service, to uncover myriad references from hundreds of journals.

At least one fee-based service (in a community college) includes signed customer accolades in the brochure: "When I needed reference material on asbestos, I got it, fast. One phone call saved me a lot of time and energy." "In a couple of hours time, a database search got me research information on computer software and hardware that would have taken me nine to ten weeks to get. When I need more research done, I'll definitely call again." And, "I needed music for a commercial I was producing. One phone call and I got what I needed. I would have been in big trouble if I couldn't have located that record."

Listing client names is effective brochure strategy. Clients in the public sector (i.e., they used tax payers' money to pay you) may be listed without client permission, although it would be courteous to ask. Permission always must be sought before listing private sector clients. Common sense will dictate those clients of whom asking permission would be inappropriate; if in doubt, don't ask and don't use their names.

Your brochure usually should not list the databases which may be accessed. If a (rare) client is sophisticated enough to want to know, that client will ask. Most clients, however, don't want to buy an ABI or an ERIC or a PSYCHINFO, and they will be put off by such a listing. What the client wants is, simply, answers to questions. A brochure should stress just that.

When brochure wording has been decided upon, the brochure must be designed and laid out. Brochure expert Chris Olson says that "an aspect of design frequently overlooked . . . is legibility," and makes the following points:[12]

1. Large amounts of text set in capital letters require more time to read than text set in lower-case letters.
2. Large blocks of text set in italic slow the reader slightly; readers prefer roman to italic type.
3. Unjustified or ragged right margin settings are read as fast as justified lines of type.
4. Reverse type, white type on a black background, slows reading by about 10%.
5. Readers prefer type faces with serifs if there is a lot of material to read. (Serifs are those little fine lines that finish off the ends of letters. . . .)
6. High-gloss papers can interfere with reading. Use dull coated papers when you know lighting conditions will cause a glare.
7. Solid, bold face type, when used repeatedly, will compete for the reader's eye. Select the message you want the reader to see first using the boldface type, then use smaller type and shading to provide visual perception of depth.

Usually the goal is to come up with a one-size-fits-all brochure, as does a Midwestern fee-based service whose "brochure is sent to all who might use services and is displayed at conferences." When designing the brochure, keep in mind what you plan to do with it. If it's going to be mailed, use a design that accommodates a mailing label and have the printer fold the brochure. (One fee-based service librarian confesses that, without any doubt, the hardest part so far of managing the service has been "Waiting for the brochure to go out and seeing what kind of response we get.")

If the brochure is going to be enclosed with letters or bills, it must be small enough to fit into a number ten-size envelope. Watch brochure weight: the final package (i.e., letter/bill plus brochure) should weigh under an ounce for domestic mailing and under a half ounce for overseas mailing: greater weight means higher postage.

If the brochure is going to be posted on bulletin boards, be sure the printer leaves some brochures unfolded. If it's going to be handed out at meetings, conventions, or exhibits, have a place on the brochure to staple a business card.

Avoid printing the brochure on paper too slick to write on. In general, it's best to avoid printing large numbers of brochures; you don't want to be stuck with brochures that need using up before you can design another. Since your services' prices may change frequently, consider printing separate price sheets as brochure attachments or enclosures.

ADVERTISING AND EXHIBITING

There are few, if any, selling modes that have not been tried by at least one fee-based service, somewhere. What works for one service, in one part of the country, may or may not work for another service elsewhere. Perhaps the only conclusion that can be drawn from this is: you will get more for your money if you concentrate on selling to a particular kind or group of customer. Going after a broad, generalized, consumer market simply does not work. Remember the selling rules: know exactly what you are going to sell, know exactly to whom you are going to sell, go where the money is, emphasize benefits and not process, and keep your sales message so simple that a nine-year-old can understand.

Paying for advertisements in magazines and newspapers is usually not cost-effective for fee-based information services. There are many reasons. Most librarians don't know how to write ads and yet do not get professional help with the job. It's even harder to write an effective ad than it is to write an effective brochure, and it's practically impossible to write a short (i.e., cheap) ad. Most short "let-us-do-your-research-for-you" kinds of advertisements draw inappropriate responses from people not prepared to pay, people who should be steered to the reference department of the nearest public library.

A librarian at a fee-based service in the Midwest writes, "We haven't set an example of making money—yet. We tried ads in several science magazines for a current awareness publication: $6,000 worth of ads got us about ten new subscribers for about $1,000 in revenues."

A service in a Southwestern state had a similar experience:

> Does it pay to advertise? In a word, no. Highest quality replies have been from a magazine geared toward small business, but it's break even at best. We find people responding to classifieds expect *immediate, guaranteed* answers for less than no money. You just can't hit any nerves in ten words or less with a scattergun approach to an unknown audience. You get so many trivial requests that it's just not worth it. I tried advertising in a popular shop magazine, and I got 30 replies per month, every month. But over 90 percent of these dealt with inconsequential things posed by people with no intention of paying $10 at most—questions such as "my neighbor's apartment was broken into, where can I buy a burglar alarm?" The few legitimate replies never added up to enough to pay for the ads.

However, for every rule there are exceptions. At least one service regularly runs an ad in its area's *Wall Street Journal* and reports that "the ad has been moderately successful." And several fee-based operations offering services useful to other libraries, such as document delivery service, regularly place classified advertisements in the magazines that librarians read. Librarians are about the only market that knows, without elaborate explanation, what "document delivery" is. The fact that these ads appear month after month, year after year, must mean that the ads are working: more money is made from the advertisements than is spent on them.

Placing advertisements in Yellow Pages also has drawn

mixed reviews. At least one fee-based service in an urban university reports that its listing in the local business-to-business Yellow Pages has been gratifyingly fruitful. Most, however, report the opposite. Not the least of the problem is to figure out which heading (or headings—a business telephone gets one "free" listing yet may pay for as many more as are appropriate) under which to be listed. Unfortunately, authorized subject headings differ from region to region in the United States; some areas now allow "Information Brokers," yet the general public usually doesn't know what an information broker is. Some fee-based services have tried "Information Bureaus," with mixed success. As one service reports, "We received a swarm of calls for concert ticket information and tourist attraction directions, but only two calls, over the period of a year, for genuine research projects." "Market Research" may be an appropriate heading in some areas, and yet the term "market research" means many things to many people, including standing on the corner of Main Street and Elm Avenue and asking how many people prefer crunchy peanut butter over smooth.

Another kind of paid advertising is radio advertising. Most fee-based services report dismal results, much of which may be attributable to condensing one's message into 30-second time slots. Success with radio may be regional, however; there have been reports that West Coast radio audiences pay more attention than do those in other parts of the country.

Exhibiting is yet another way of getting business, and more than a handful of fee-based services report gratifying results. As an exhibitor, you contract for booth space in the exhibits section of a commercial, association, or professional meeting and then pray that enough customers will be attracted to your booth to offset the usually large expense involved. (If your fee-based service is in a nonprofit institution, such as a university or a hospital, reduced rates may be available to you.)

When deciding whether or not to exhibit, do not let yourself be influenced by the pressure you will get from booth-space sellers. Think carefully about who will be attending the exhibits and ask questions: do attendees really include decision makers—the money spenders—in your targeted market?

As an exhibitor you are obligated to be in attendance in your booth at all times during exhibits hours, and you will sign a contact agreeing to this. Your contract will also specify for what booth-furnishing items you are paying—the chair, carpet, and table all have their price. The more expensive booths are those closest to the bar and along critical pathways. You may ask to be located next to, or far from, specific other exhibitors. Even though it may seem expensive, stay in or near the exhibits hotel—you'll want to use your room during the day for respite and refills, and at night for easy storage of supplies and equipment. Off-hours security in some exhibits areas can be marginal.

When exhibiting, stay on your feet—no one ever sold much sitting down. Look interested, even if you are bored. If you have a computer for demonstration, set things up so your back is not to the aisle and audience as you key-in a search. Don't allow one customer to engage your total attention for more than a few minutes; make a date to see that person later, after exhibits close, and turn to other booth visitors. Have plenty of business cards and brochures. Smile.

Exhibiting is not for everyone. And yet fee-based information services have profitably exhibited at engineering meetings, law associations, automobile conventions, and more. The fee-based service in the science division of an inner city library exhibited at an inventors' show and drew copious attention by demonstrating online patent searching. Unless other librarians are significant customers of your service, be wary of committing money and time to exhibiting at library-related meetings. Certainly your booth will attract interest from your peers, but will it attract business?

DIRECT MAIL

Direct mail appears to be consistently successful as a method of finding customers for a fee-based service. As one

person says: "Why? Because you can include a lot of information on one or more pages that give potential clients a quick
picture of what you do." Unlike most advertising, direct mail
can give recipients enough data so they can easily determine if
and how they might become customers. In marketing jargon,
they "qualify themselves," they are "qualified leads."

Direct mail involves sending a piece of mail—letter,
brochure, pictures, samples, return postcard, etc.—to prospects on the premise that some percent of those prospects will
become customers. How large that percent will be, and how
large the average incoming job will be, is hard to predict. As a
general rule, a "good" list will yield 1 percent to 1.5 percent—
i.e., mailing to 1,000 prospects should uncover 10 to 15 new
customers.

What list to use, of course, depends on to whom the fee-
based service has decided to sell. Some lists may be available inhouse. For example, a university will have lists of
alumni, trustees, and donors. A hospital will have lists of
affiliated physicians and benefactors. An institution's public relations department may have appropriate lists. What
percent of people on these lists will become customers is hard
to predict at first; one might hope for a higher than one
percent yield from people already familiar with your institution. The best list, of course, is made up of wealthy, busy
people who need a lot of information on many different topics,
often.

Almost every conceivable kind of list can be bought from
list brokers—contact them for mailing list catalogs. Lists of
engineers, for instance, can be broken down by specialty (8,009
pollution control engineers), by geography (1,894 aeronautic
and astro engineers in Texas), by affiliation (2,095 aquatic and
marine scientists in education), by title (6,127 CEOs or presi-
dents who happen to be engineers, too), or by age (5,696
between 40 and 50). List costs are both variable and negotiable,
usually running between $.04 and $.25 per name. Before
buying a list, inquire how the list was made up and try to
satisfy yourself as far as you can as to the list's integrity.
Librarians in one fee-based service wanted to buy a list of

public libraries and asked a list broker how its list had been compiled. The reply was that Yellow Pages had been consulted, nationwide. Since the librarians knew that many public libraries are not listed in the Yellow Pages, they shopped elsewhere for a better list.

Lists can be delivered in almost any format; most direct mailers without sophisticated specialized mail-handling equipment purchase names on self-stick labels. Virtually all lists are bought for one-time use only, and list brokers monitor this vigilantly; once you stick a label on an envelope and mail it out, that name is "lost" to you until or unless there is a reply. The list of those who reply, however, is yours to manage as you wish. Gradually your fee-based service will build up its own mailing list of prospects, current customers, and ex-customers, and you can create your own self-stick labels for future mailings.

Prepare whatever is to be mailed with great care (use suggestions in the section on brochures). If possible, get help from someone who has direct mail experience. If your mail piece involves a tear-off portion which is to be mailed back to you, be sure that your name, complete address and telephone number appear both on what is torn off and on the portion retained by your prospect. Time your mailing so it is received on a Tuesday, and your message will receive better attention than on Mondays (things are piled high from the weekend) or on Thursdays or Fridays (getting ready for the weekend). Wednesdays are almost as good as Tuesdays, but not quite.

If a direct mailing is ineffective, keep trying but change only one element at a time (either the mail piece or the list) or you won't learn which element of your efforts worked and which didn't. If a certain list is successful, buy the same list again and use it six months later: you will get virtually the same percentage of new customers.

How many direct mail pieces to send out at a time depends on your budget (experience recommends first class over bulk mail), your arrangements for stuffing and stamping, and how many replies you and your staff are prepared to handle at a time. There is no point in sending out 5,000 pieces at once if you cannot handle 50 replies (1%) virtually simultaneously. However, it probably makes sense to *buy* at least 5,000 names at a time, as it costs fewer pennies per name in larger quantities.

As you gain experience in using direct mail, you will be able to forecast results—i.e., your sales—with surprising accuracy. You can plot your calendar: start planning in December, mail 2,000 in April, 20 new customers by June, mail 2,000 in May, 20 more customers by July, plus a repeat or two from June and possibly some referrals, and so on throughout the year.

MARKETING WITHIN: CHARGEBACKS

Virtually every selling, marketing, and public relations ploy discussed above is being used by corporate special librarians responsible for charging back for library services within the parent institution—whether the chargebacks are to departments, projects, proposals, individuals, or to clients of the firm.

In most cases, a brochure is invaluable. Typical comment: "Our brochure is routinely given to new staff members, and a library tour is part of their orientation." A brochure for a large utility company points out that the library is "XYZ's answer to the information explosion," and points out the specific benefit that "our XYZ focus enables us to organize information into the most useful targeted format for XYZ managers." The brochure stresses that "one phone call gives XYZ managers access" to research and consulting services, inhouse newsletters and reports, current awareness "information packages," electronic news briefs, public access databases, etc.

In another example, the format of the "brochure" for libraries in a world-wide manufacturing conglomerate is six pages three-hole-punched for insertion in the company's "World Headquarters Service Directory." Page one is a chart showing what functions and services are the information center's responsibilities. In this case, five units report to the information center: library services, library systems, the business library, the technical library, and one other special-purpose library. Managers' names and telephone extensions are given.

Page two gives specific directions on how to get to each library and their hours of operation (example: "Always open, staff on duty 8:00 a.m. - 4:30 p.m. Monday-Friday, enter by lobby during nonworking hours with pass or by special arrangement"). Specifics are given regarding where to go and whom to call about services, such as Annual Reports, Photo Library, Contents Previews, Translations, and Research Notebooks.

The following brochure pages give easy-to-scan details about:

- "What We Have," which covers everything from books to safety data sheets, standards/specifications, unpublished technical reports, photos of people and products and plants),
- "How and Where You Find Them in the Information Center," which ranges from searching the inhouse database to asking for staff assistance,
- "What's New—Publications You Can Receive at Your Desk," which includes a listing of new publications and subscriptions, patents previews, new translations, etc.
- "Explanatory Notes" clarifies what may be borrowed and for how long and in what format, how quickly staff can respond to various requests, etc.

The brochure's last page details special services such as training for those who want to do their own online searching and how requests for new material are handled.

In an office of a large international accounting firm, virtually all library services are charged back, and most of what is charged back is then charged out to the firm's customers. According to the brochure, library service is also made available directly to outside customers: "We invite clients and alumni to use our information services." The librarian who manages the information center writes, "I exist in a fee-based world so charging for information is expected. . . . If you work for an institution, doesn't it expect to recover some of the costs? Is it really a hard sell? Or is my experience very unusual?"

The information services brochure for this library can be described as "understated." The brochure is pocket-size, printed on heavy glossy paper, and contains less than 1,000 words spread over four 3 by 8 inch pages. Page one summarizes the company's approach to solving business problems which "requires a general knowledge of the business world and a specific knowledge of each client's business" and outlines development over almost a century of the company's national and regional information centers. The balance of the brochure talks about:

- Principal components of information center services (professional staff experience, access to other research libraries via professional courtesy, access to databases)
- What is in this information center
- How company offices and libraries abroad make information available
- The six databases most in demand
- Five subjects which are among those for which the information center provides monthly abstracts

A final statement concludes: "We believe that current, complete information contributes to productivity and that a lack of information is an expense no business can tolerate."

A regular, or even an occasional, newsletter can serve as a selling tool. One such newsletter features the "10 hottest questions of the month," another spotlights the "Question of the Year." One corporate library sends out a newsletter-type memo whenever a new database or application of a database, becomes available: "New [that magic word!] for you from your library!"

When selling library service inhouse, soliciting and keeping fan mail can be useful. An example is demonstrated by the corporate library brochure which quotes this accolade: "My customer was impressed that QRS can be so knowledgeable about industry issues. . . . [The library] really does enhance our credibility." Another example from industry: "The published

products of the . . . [library] are notable in this company for
their dependability."

A special librarian in a fast-growing communications
company says, "I have made use of an evaluation form that I
send out with every response to a reference request. Some
responses have been great—'This helped me make a $6 million
sale,' 'I think the library is one of the best resources this
company has.' I would have never heard from these people
without the evaluation form."

This particular "Library Reference Request Evaluation"
form opens with, "Your evaluation of this reference request will
greatly assist us in maintaining high-quality information
services. Please complete this form and return it as soon as
possible for our review." Among the questions asked are: Was
the delivery time reasonable? What percentage of the material
was useful to you? Did the material answer your question? Will
the information from this reference request assist you in making a business decision or completing a sale?

Corporate librarians, as well as managers of fee-based
services for outside customers, have conducted market-re-
search-type surveys as part of efforts to "sell" the library.
The survey can be conducted using interviews, through a
questionnaire, or by electronic mail. In-house market surveys attempt to pinpoint staff information needs—what kind
of information is needed, how quickly is it needed, in what
form is it needed, and how does staff procure the information
now? Answers to these questions can guide a service's development and can make future charge-backs for library services
infinitely easier to establish and defend. (The accounting firm
library whose brochure is described above was designed and
developed around a market survey carried out almost 20 years
ago.)

Word of mouth can work well when marketing information
services inhouse: "Marketing is really done *for* us by the use
partners have made of our services—they tell new people how
to use us." A report from a large, multi-site corporation says,
"The librarian markets research services to the staff through
company newsletters and inhouse workshops; we always try

to look at our service from the customers' viewpoint, and our customers are our firms' executives."

Literature on how to market the concept of charging back for library services within an institution is sparse. Two newsletters published by librarians, *MLS* and *Marketing Treasures*,[13] give specific, hands-on hints. *Marketing Treasures* periodically sends "Cut and Paste" graphics sheets, and original artwork in camera-ready form, which can be duplicated at will. The book *Marketing the Modern Information Center: A Guide to Intrapreneurship for the Information Manager*[14] surveys six information managers who are "active self promoters," and addresses marketing issues in the corporate setting.

A few marketing-specific workshops and courses are available to librarians faced with selling the concept of charging back for information services. *Marketing Treasures* lists upcoming seminars in "The Crystal Ball" section of the newsletter. A handful of library schools have offered short-term (usually one week) marketing courses. Special Libraries Association, Medical Libraries Association, Information Industry Association[15] and similar societies have sponsored marketing courses.

References

1. Michael DeBakey, M.D., "When your doctor needs to know—fast," *Reader's Digest*, July 1987, pp. 110-113, is an excellent example of generic publicity in a widely read public magazine.
2. Erik Mortensen, "Tap Into Info Power—create profits for your company through knowledge management," *Administrative Management*, November 1987, pp. 29, is both substantial and easy to understand.
3. Judi Sovner-Ribbler, "Which database solves which marketing problem? What you need to know about the 10 most useful online databases that offer sales, marketing and management support," *Sales and Marketing Management*, July 1988, pp. 53-55. Includes a section on "What is a database, anyway?" and another on alternative online services.
4. Katherine Ackerman, "The Subject is: BUSINESS—an update

on electronic information sources," *American Libraries*, May 1987, pp. 378+.

5. Tina Roose, "Computer Indexes vs. Print Indexes," *Library Journal*, 1 September 1987, pp. 158-159.

6. Tim Miller, "Confessions of an Online Fanatic," *Information Today*, September 1987, pp. 22-25.

7. For specific suggestions on how to do a good job at being visible, check "The Power of Personal Publicity," *Working Woman*, February 1988, pp. 48-50. It provides suggestions on how to get noticed: become active in professional associations, volunteer to write the newsletter, work on committees, speak. Specifically addresses "how to get good PR in a bad situation" and how to talk to the press.

8. For suggestions on how to deal with creating a positive image, check the cassette tape recording "Image Builders: Personal Management and Image Building Skills for Information Professionals," written and narrated by Kaycee Hale, Executive Director of the Fashion Institute of Design & Merchandising (FIDM) and sponsored by Special Libraries Association and FIDM. Available from FIDM Productions, 818 W. Seventh St., Los Angeles, CA 90017.

9. For specific suggestions on how to set the stage for and manage an interview see Jeffrey P. Geibel's "60 Minutes Is Here! How to handle the press," *MicroEconomics*, May 1987, pp. 10-11. Describes how to assemble "media kits"—background information, photographs, brochures—to help an interviewer ask appropriate questions.

10. This section on brochures is an expansion of a talk given by the author. See pp. 12-14, "Selling the service," in *Fee-Based Services: Issues & Answers*, cited in note 1, Chapter Two.

11. At current writing, the most easily-obtained information about desktop publishing is available from those who seek to have you buy their brand. A general discussion is available from Franklynn Peterson and Judi K-Turkel who write a syndicated column called *The Business Computer*. Their "Making publishing cents" is a brand-name-free introduction to desktop publishing and was first published in March 1988. Copies of this column and others (including "Cheaper Desktop Publishing Route") in the series are available for a modest fee from the authors at The Business Computer, 4343 West Beltline Highway, Madison, Wisconsin 53711.

Online magazine monitors desktop publishing via its column "Journal Watch" and alerts readers to articles such as Dominic R. D'Acquisto's "10 Hot Desktop Publishing Tips" in MACazine, February 1988, pp. 64-67.

12. From the column "Promotion Gems" in *Marketing Treasures*, November 1987, p. 3. See below for information on availability of *Marketing Treasures*.

13. *MLS* (8 issues a year) is published by Riverside Data Inc., Harrod's Creek, KY 40027, and is edited by Sharon LaRosa, Box 2286, Abington, MA 02351, 617-871-6288. *Marketing Treasures* (bimonthly) is published and edited by Chris Olson of Chris Olson & Associates, 857 Twin Harbor Dr., Arnold, MD 21012, 301-647-6708. *MLS* published a two-part article, "Marketing the fee-based service," by Debra Schneider, in the September 1988 and October 1988 issues.

14. Janet Schmidt, *Marketing the Modern Information Center: A Guide to Intrapreneurship for the Information Manager*, [1987]. Available from FIND/SVP, 625 Ave. of the Americas, New York, NY 10011, 800-346-3787 (in NY 212-645-4500).

15. Among the organizations that have sponsored workshops on marketing/selling are:

- Special Libraries Association, 1700 18th St., NW, Washington, DC 20009.
- Medical Library Association, 919 N. Michigan Avenue #3208, Chicago, IL 60611, 312-266-2456.
- Information Industry Association, 555 New Jersey Ave., NW, #800, Washington, DC 20001.

Afterword

This book has attempted to serve as an introduction to the growing phenomenon of charging fees for library services. The current situation has been described: What is happening about fee-charging *now* in academic libraries, in public libraries, in special libraries? What about charging back and charging out? How do people feel about it all?

The answers to these questions as described here neither condemn nor condone charging fees. The attempt has been merely to paint an up-to-date picture, as far as that picture can now be determined. Each reader must decide the whether and the how of fee charging. No single answer or method is right—or wrong.

The section on planning is designed to help not only those who have decided to go ahead with a fee-based service. It also is designed for those exploring what tasks need tackling should such a decision be made. Being informed, knowing what's involved, is a crucial part of decision making.

The material on selling should help those still on the fence, and yet its primary goal is to give those already engulfed in fee-based activity some hands-on, practical suggestions for selling. Such details are hard to find in the main body of library literature and most fee-based librarians need all the selling help they can get.

Sprinkled throughout this book are suggestions on how to find out more about various facets and ramifications of charging fees for library services. New items appear all the time, of course, and yet the notes section to each chapter here should

serve to get readers started in getting the information they
need.

What are the author's conclusions?

- There is fee-free paranoia out there.
- This book merely scratches the surface of a complex question.
- Fee-based services in various guises are springing up everywhere.
- Wonderfully talented people are grappling with the resulting is-
  sues and problems, and are for the most part coping virtually alone.
- Misinformation abounds, communication is weak. Wheels are being
  reinvented nationwide.

What's next on the agenda? How can we help each other?
How can we deal with the fees issues from a position of
strength? There's work for us all. We need continuing dialog in
all sectors of our profession.

- Those who are operating successful fee-based services (you know
  who you are) must somehow carve out time to write jargon-free
  how-to-do it guides to implementing and *managing* fee-based
  services. Don't tell us your "trade secrets" if you feel you shouldn't,
  yet tell us what you can. You'll save yourselves trouble in the long
  run—fewer of us will be chasing you for advice.
- Special librarians and others who charge back and/or charge out
  need to write down, in simple language, their acquired wisdom. You
  needn't share proprietary information—almost any guidance would
  help.
- Those who have made mistakes in coping with fee-based issues
  might have the grace to share, in writing, what happened, what
  they have learned. We'll learn too.
- Our schools of library and information science might somehow fit
  into crowded schedules something about fee-charging and what it
  involves. (Of course, if more were written on the subject it would be
  easier to teach!)
- We should continue to create continuing education opportunities—
  both within our associations and outside of them—for those who
  want to teach and those who want to learn. (Good news is that a
  third full-scale conference on fee-based services in academic
  libraries is in the wind for the early 1990s.)
- A published collection of forms (both paper and software adapta-

tions) would be useful. Forms used to manage one fee-based service can well be adapted to others.

- Public libraries must continue to champion and protect the rights of *all* people. There are, obviously, many shades of grey between the black and the white, between the fee and the free.

GOOD LUCK!

Index

Academic libraries, 15–20
  references, 36–39
Accounting, 57–61
Accounts receivable, 56
Action plans, 88–90
Advertising, 128–130
  definition of, 100
  direct mail, 131–134
  free, 113
  radio, 130
  references, 110, 111
  where to place, 129
  word-of-mouth, 102, 137,
    138
American Libraries, 115,
American Library Association,
  62, 74
Annual reports, 117
Articles, 114–116
  generic, 118
Association libraries, 27–29,
  101
Attitudes, 5, 17, 33, 56, 57, 90
  references, 11, 12

Benefits to clients, 108, 109,
  124, 125
Billable time, 35
Billing forms, 61
Billing methods, 56–61

Billing out. *see* Charging out
Brochures, 121–129
  internal, 134–136
BRS, 59
Budgets, 88–90
  academic, 19–20
  in other service departments,
    94
  promotion, 62
  startup, 61–63
Business market, 51

Capital equipment, 55, 62
CCC (Copyright Clearance
  Center), 76, 77
CD-ROM databases, 4, 21
Changeover, 90–97
Charge backs, 29–34
  billing methods, 31
  changing to, 90–97
  indexing services, 32
  interpretations of, 91
  marketing, 134–138
  planning for, 90–97
    homework, 93–94
  references, 97
  rates, 30
Charging out, 34–36, 135, 136
  planning for, 90–97
Checklists

brochures, 122, 123
charge-back planning, 93–94
proposals, 87–89
Churchill, Winston, 107
Client benefits, 108, 109, 124, 125
Client goals, 47
Clients
  communicating with, 96
  identifying, 50–53, 71
  listing in brochures, 126
  market research for, 49
Collections, 56
Columns, 116
Commercial copying, 77, 78
Communicating with clients, 96
Communicating with management, 34
Communications tools, 49
Competing fee-based services, 50
Competitor intelligence service, 50
Conclusions, 143
Consulting rate, rule of thumb, 68, 69
Continuing education, 143
Copying, 77, 78
Copyright, 76–81
  references, 85, 86
Copyright Clearance Center (CCC), 76, 77, 80
Copyright Law of 1976, 77, 78, 81
Copyright Law of 1986, 79
Corporate libraries, 23, 24, 30–36, 102
Cost centers, 47, 48, 95
Cost recovery, 30, 31, 47, 48, 95
Crusading, 109

Customer mix, 50
Customers. see headings beginning with Client

Databases
  CD-ROM, 4, 21
  not listing in brochures, 127
Demand analysis, 52
Departmental budgets, 94
Design of forms, 61
Design of brochures, 127, 128
DIALOG, 59
Dialorder, 57
Direct costs, 30, 31, 91, 92
Direct mail, 131–134
Disclaimers
  copyright, 80, 81
  liability for errors, 74
Document delivery
  electronic mail orders, 57
  liability for copyright violations, 78–79
  planning for, 49
  rates, 66
Easy selling, 104, 105
Education, 142
80-20 rule, 104, 105
Electronic mail
  for clients, 49
  orders, 57
Entrepreneurism, 1, 2
  references, 11
Equipment planning and budgeting, 55, 62
Errors insurance, 73
Ethical issues, 72
  of fee charging, 2–4
  references, 11–14, 83
Exhibiting, 130, 131
Exhibits in proposals, 89

External charges. *see* Charging
   out

Fair use, 77, 78
Fan mail, 119, 136, 137
Fast-growth companies, 32, 33
Fee-based service directories,
   13, 14
Fee charging
   attitudes, 5, 17, 33, 56, 57, 90
   making the decision, 4–6
   who does it, 6–10
   see also Charge backs;
      Charging Out
Fee structures, 9, 10, 63–70
   academic libraries, 18
   case history, 66–69
   medical libraries, 25, 26
   public libraries, 22
   references, 82, 83
   simple, 65
Ferraro, Geraldine, 118–119
Financial goals, 47
Forecasting, 71
Forms design, 61
Free access to information, 2, 3
Free advertising, 113
Free service to all, 46

Generic publicity, 117–119
Goals, 44–48
   public libraries, 22, 46
Gradual changeover, 95

Hiring, 54
Hold-harmless clause, 74
Holidays, 71
Hospital libraries, 24–27
Hours of operation, 70, 71

Identifying clients, 50–53, 71

IFLA (International Federation
   of Library Associations), 20
Image, 120
Indexing services charges, 32
Information Industry
   Association, 140
Information-related products,
   8
Information sharing, 142
Insurance, 73, 74
   references, 84
Internal charges. *see* Charge
   back
Internal marketing, 134–138
International Federation of
   Library Associations
   (IFLA), 20
Interviews
   market research, 52
   media, 121
Intrapreneurism, 1, 2

Jargon, 106, 123, 124
Journal vouchers, 60

Knowing your organization, 93

Labor costs, 65
Land Grant colleges, 72
Language
   in brochures, 123, 124
   in selling, 105, 106
   speeches, 120
Law libraries, references, 41
Lending policies, 49
Lending rates, 66
Liability, 73, 74
   copyright law, 78, 79
   references, 84
Library budget, 93–94
Library jargon, 106, 123, 124

Library of Congress subject headings, 106

Mail advertising, 131–134
Mailing lists, 132, 133
Mailing techniques, 133, 134
Market research, 52
  as a *Yellow Pages* heading, 130
  for clients, 49
  internal, 137
Marketing plan, 50–53
Marketing surveys, 52, 53
Marketing, 101–104
  definition of, 100
  internal, 134–138
  references, 81, 82, 138–140
  workshops on, 138
Media interviews, 121
Medical libraries, 24–27
Medical Library Association, 140
  references, 40, 41
Money management, 56–61

Naming the service, 53
National Small Business United (SBU), 110
News releases, 113, 114
Newsletters, 116, 117, 136
Non-affiliated patrons, 6
  in academic libraries, 15
  lending to, 49, 66
Noncommercial copying, 79
Not-for-profit status, 74–76
  references, 84, 85
Notice of copyright, 79

Office supplies, 62
Olson, Christine, 127

Online search services
  planning, 49
Organizational awareness, 93
Organizational planning, 53
Out-of-pocket expenses, 30, 31, 91, 92

Pay as you go, 3
Photocopying, 77, 78
Physical space planning, 55
Planning, 43–86
  basic issues, 43, 44
  references, 81–86
Presentations as a selling tool, 103
Press releases, 113, 114
Pressure, 10
Pricing. *see* Rate setting
Products sold, 8
Profit centers, 47, 48
Profit vs. not-for-profit, 74–76
Promotion budget, 62
Proposals, 87–90
Public libraries, 20–24
  goals, 22, 46
  references, 39, 40
Public relations, 100
Publicity
  free, 113
  generic, 117–118
Publishing, 114–116, 143

Radio advertising, 130
Rate setting, 9, 10, 63–70
  academic libraries, 18
  case history, 66–69
  hospital libraries, 25, 26
  public libraries, 22
  references, 82, 83
Receivables, 56
Recordkeeping, 55, 96

and accounting, 57–61
  see also Statistics
Referrals, 105
Remote clients, 51
Repeat customers, 104, 105
Research services, 32
  planning for, 49
Resource sharing, 3
Response time, 50, 51
Restrictions on service, 72
Revenues, 57–61

SBA (United States Small
  Business Administration),
  99, 100, 110
SBU (National Small Business
  United), 110
Scheduling, 54, 70, 71
SCORE (Service Corps of
  Retired Executives), 110
Selling, 99–111
  definition of, 100
  easy, 104, 105
  not selling, 103
  principles of, 105–109
  references, 110, 138–140
  seminars and workshops, 99,
    100, 110
  to decision makers, 87–90
  to library staff, 90
Seminars on selling, 99, 100,
  110
Service Corps of Retired
  Executives (SCORE), 110
Service objectives, 45, 46
Services offered, 7–8
  academic libraries, 15
  planning for, 48–50
Setting rates. see Rate setting
Sharing expertise, 143
Simple fee structures, 65

Simple language, 107
Small Business Administration
  (SBA), 99–100, 110
Space planning, 55
Special libraries, 23, 24
  charging out, 30–36
  marketing and selling, 102
Special Libraries Association,
  140
Speeches, 120, 121
Staff attitudes, 5, 33, 36, 90
Staff planning, 53–55
Staff scheduling, 54, 70, 71
Startups
  academic, 16–18
  budgets, 61–63
  startup time, 63
Statistics, 94, 95
  see also Recordkeeping
Stress factor, 10
Subject heading, language, 106
Subsidies, 63
Support staff, 54
Surveys, 52, 53

Tax-exempt institutions, 74–
  76
  references, 84, 85
Telephoning for clients, 49
Testimonials, 119, 126, 136,
  137
  see also Word-of-mouth
    advertising
Time sheets, 35
Trade association libraries, 27–
  29
Turnaround time, 50, 51

United States Chamber of
  Commerce, 110

United States Small Business
    Administration (SBA), 99,
    100, 110
United Technologies Inc., 107

VendaCard system, 29
Visibility, 119, 120

Wall St. Journal
    advertisements, 129
Warning about charge backs,
    96
Who's Who, 119
Word-of-mouth advertising,
    102, 137, 138
    see also Testimonials

Workshops
    on marketing, 138, 140
    on selling, 99, 100, 110
Writing
    advertisements, 107
    articles, 114–116
    brochures, 121–126, 134–
        136
    columns, 116
    news releases, 113, 114
    newsletters, 116–117,
        136
    proposals, 87–90

Yellow Pages, 129–30, 133